D1031633

THE LITERARY MICROCOSM

THEORIES OF INTERPRETATION
OF THE LATER NEOPLATONISTS

COLUMBIA STUDIES
IN THE
CLASSICAL TRADITION

under the direction of

WILLIAM V. HARRIS (Editor) — W. T. H. JACKSON
PAUL OSKAR KRISTELLER — WALTHER LUDWIG

VOLUME II

LEIDEN
E. J. BRILL
1976

B 517
C 65

THE LITERARY MICROCOSM

THEORIES OF INTERPRETATION OF THE LATER NEOPLATONISTS

BY

JAMES A. COULTER

DISCARDED
URI LIBRARY

LEIDEN

E. J. BRILL

1976

Columbia Studies in the Classical Tradition *publishes monographs by members of the Columbia University faculty and by former Columbia students. Its subjects are the following: Greek and Latin literature, ancient philosophy, Greek and Roman history, classical archaeology, and the influence of the classical tradition on mediaeval, Renaissance and modern cultures.*

The publication of this book was aided by a grant from the Stanwood Cockey Lodge Foundation.

ISBN 90 04 04489 2

© *1976 by The Trustees of Columbia University in the City of New York*

All rights reserved. No part of this book may be reproduced or translated in any form, by print, photoprint, microfilm, microfiche or any other means without written permission from the publisher

PRINTED IN THE NETHERLANDS

99842

TER RECENSIE

CONTENTS

Foreword VII

Introduction I

I. The Three Streams 5
   1. The Three Streams 5
   2. Genre Criticism 7
   3. Ethical Criticism 9
   4. Allegorical Criticism 19

II. Mimesis: Eicon and Symbol 32
   1. Plato and Aristotle 32
   2. Neoplatonic Contributions 39
      Appendix I: *Symbolon* 60
      Appendix II: Symbol and Metaphor 68

III. Unity: The Many and the One 73
   1. Classical and Post-Classical Antecedents 73
   2. Unity in Neoplatonic Exegesis 77

IV. Organicism: The Microcosmic Analogue 95
   1. Sources of Literary Organicism 95
   2. Neoplatonic Contributions 101
   3. The Poet in Neoplatonic Theory 103
   4. Poetic Matter and Style in Neoplatonic Theory . . . 120

Conclusion 127

Appendix: Greek Texts of the Neoplatonic Commentators . . 131

Bibliography 142

Index of Passages 146

FOREWORD

It has been my aim in this study to cast light upon some little known achievements in the history of ancient literary thought. One does not readily think of the Neoplatonists as *literary* theorists, but I hope I have shown that, at least in their commentaries on the dialogues of Plato, they did speculate often, and at times with great fruitfulness, on fundamental problems relating to the interpretation of literary texts. These commentators, especially Proclus, surely merit a more secure place in the history of literary criticism and theory than they now occupy, and I shall be happy if my study makes some contribution toward achieving that end.

Certain aspects of my task were rendered easier, or at least more enjoyable, by the fact that there are relatively few secondary studies on the exegetical theories and techniques of the later Neoplatonists. I was therefore able to proceed unencumbered by the constant need to weigh my own views against previous work, a freedom which a scholar who has written, let us say, on Homer or Vergil will most likely envy. On the other hand, it is also true that I have been for the most part without the kind of guidance which might have saved me from blunders I feel sure I have committed. A happy sense of breaking partially new ground has thus been clouded by the anxieties which beset the worker in a relatively undeveloped field of scholarship.

This is not to imply that I have been without benefit of scholarly help of another kind. The editors of the *Columbia Studies in the Classical Tradition*, who were good enough to consider my monograph for inclusion in that series, also read it with care, and it is with pleasure that I take this opportunity to express my gratitude for help to Professors William Harris, William Jackson, Paul Kristeller, and Walther Ludwig of Columbia University. Professor Kristeller, especially, with his wide knowledge of ancient philosophy, helped me to avoid a good number of pitfalls and downright errors. I also wish to thank Professors Malcolm Brown and Seth Schein for thoughtful criticisms. For errors which remain I am, obviously, solely accountable. My colleagues' advice has more often than not been thankfully heeded, but the work remains, for better or worse, my own.

Grateful acknowledgement is also due the following scholarly bodies for subsidies which allowed me to devote a sabbatical year in 1970-1971 to preliminary research for the present work: to the Guggenheim Foundation for a Fellowship; to the American Council of Learned Societies for a Grant-in-Aid; to the Council for Research in the Humanities of Columbia University for a Summer Research Grant.

October, 1974, New York City   J.A.C.

INTRODUCTION

The present volume is a study of the extant commentaries on a number of Plato's dialogues which were written by Neoplatonist philosophers of the fifth and sixth centuries A.D. in Athens and Alexandria. The term Neoplatonist, which is of modern origin, denotes a group of thinkers, beginning with Plotinus (205-270 A.D.), who saw themselves not as *Neo*platonists, but as Platonists pure and simple, faithful to the fundamental doctrines of their Master. In presenting my conclusions about their commentaries my aim has been to make more generally known a body of doctrines which, in my view, make up a significant chapter in the history of Western thought on literature and literary interpretation. While writing this volume I have had always in mind those readers, whether classicists or not, whose interests lie in the broader history of literary criticism and theory and in the recurrent problems which have exercised critics and theorists from Plato to the present day. My book is therefore, necessarily and intentionally, rather general in character, and I lay no claim, at least in a primary way, to its being a contribution to the specialized study of ancient Neoplatonism. It is, instead, an examination of the Neoplatonists' contribution to the solution of certain perennial difficulties in literary theory and interpretation. In accordance with this aim, I have adopted a number of policies which might otherwise have seemed inappropriate. First, I have everywhere attempted to present the relevant classical background to the major critical problems which were confronted in the Neoplatonist commentaries; this has turned out to be chiefly a reexamination of the fundamental arguments advanced early in the tradition by Plato and Aristotle. This has not always been so, however, and in a number of instances the contributions of later thinkers are also discussed. Much of this matter is already familiar to fellow classicists, and to others as well, but I hope that some, at least, of my formulations concerning the literary theories of Plato and Aristotle will contain an element of novelty and suggestiveness. In any event, the retrospective portion of each chapter is presented in what is admittedly a dogmatic fashion, since it was clear that any attempt to take serious issue with differing views on troublesome points of interpretation would have enlarged the book in a way which seemed inappropriate. I have also made a point of citing in my notes relevant studies of which the specialist will not need to be reminded, but which are not necessarily part of the scholarly apparatus of the non-classicist. Lastly, I have everywhere provided translations of the Greek and Latin texts under discussion. I have occasionally used published translations, but in most cases the translations are my own. I believe that in this matter even fellow Hellenists will be occasionally grateful for guidance, however inadequate, in unravelling the meaning of these often remarkably obscure writers. For those curious to consult the not always easily obtainable originals of translated passages from Neoplatonist commentaries, I have provided an appendix of Greek texts.

Two matters remain. The first has to do with the relationship between, on the one hand, the allegorical techniques of interpretation which formed the background to the theoretical discoveries and practical exegetical procedures discussed in the present volume and, on the other, those modes of Christian allegorization which were increasingly in evidence from the end of the first century on. That such a relationship existed (all but completely in the direction of borrowing by the Christians) is a matter generally agreed upon by scholars and is a much-discussed episode in the history of Western thought. Nonetheless it is a subject which must be excluded from the scope of the present study. For however great the intrinsic merits of such an investigation may be, and however clear a scholarly imperative it is, in theory, to treat significant developments in later ancient thought in a way which transcends the often unjustifiable barriers erected by modern scholarship between the pagan and Christian traditions, an endeavor of such a magnitude lies outside both the intention and the scholarly powers of the author. In any event, my own impression is that although much can be demonstrated about Neoplatonic influences on Christian thought, very little in the matter of reverse influence has been, or can be, shown to be the case. For this reason, if for no other, an omission of any but passing consideration of Christian allegorization seems justified in what is primarily a study of the achievement of the Neoplatonists. It is also true that a scholarly account of the influence of Neoplatonic ideas on subsequent critical theory would be a welcome contribution, but this, too, unfortunately, would require another, far more ambitious kind of endeavor than I am ready or equipped to undertake. For those readers, however, who already possess some familiarity with medieval Christian exegesis, or with critical theories of the Renaissance or the Romantic period, the line of descent from thinkers like Proclus will, I think, be self-evident.

There is another point of scholarly procedure which requires comment. Ancient Neoplatonism, although distinct enough from other philosophical movements of later antiquity, was, viewed from within, far from being a system of monolithic uniformity. The doctrines of third-century thinkers like Numenius and Plotinus were, in many important respects, different from those of Proclus and other later Neoplatonists. The reader may therefore, at times, be justifiably puzzled about the precise paternity of doctrines which I characterize as, in a general way, "Neoplatonic." In this matter the specific texts under examination have determined my procedure. In the great majority of cases it is the commentaries of Proclus which I have subjected to more extended analysis, with Hermeias of Alexandria, his approximate contemporary, a far second. Olympiodorus and other commentators will, on occasion, be referred to, but their derivative and woodenly scholastic commentaries rarely contain anything of interest, at least for the purposes of this study. Accordingly, in much that I have written by way of philosophical background to the exegetical principles of the Neoplatonists, whatever bears the label Neoplatonic may generally be taken to refer to the doctrines of Proclus. This is a reasonable procedure, and not only because of the specific reasons just set forth; it possesses additional validity in that Proclus, on account both of the date at which he lived and his own philosophical temperament, became the great systematizer of ancient Neoplatonism. He therefore, more than any other, can justifiably be thought of as the "spokesman" for the general doctrines of that movement. Where it is important to distinguish the contributions of a specific thinker, as I do, for example, with Iamblichus, he is of course referred to by name. Doxographical blurrings no doubt remain, but I genuinely believe that they in no real way impair the special aims of my investigation.

Finally, the reader will probably find it useful to have before his eyes a list of the commentaries which are discussed in the following pages. The texts will be listed according to author and Platonic dialogue which is the subject of the commentary; dates of commentators, whether approximate or exact, are included in parentheses. Fuller and more precise citations can be found in the bibliography:

Damascius of Athens (ca. 458-after 533 A.D.)
   Philebus
Hermeias of Alexandria (middle of 5th century A.D.)
   Phaedrus
Olympiodorus of Alexandria (second half of 6th century A.D.)
   Gorgias
   Phaedo
Proclus of Athens (410-485 A.D.)
   First Alcibiades
   Cratylus
   Parmenides
   Republic
   Timaeus

CHAPTER ONE

THE THREE STREAMS

I. THE THREE STREAMS

It can be argued, and indeed has been, that there are two fundamental modes of literary criticism.[1] In the one, the criteria by which a literary work is deemed "good" or "bad," a "success" or "failure," are, as a matter of general tendency, sought somewhere outside the work itself. In the other the critic's goal is thought instead to be the discovery of the natural or inherent forms of a given genre or conventional literary structure. From this second perspective a specific work will be more or less successful to the degree that it actualizes the ends or final form implicit in the genre to which it belongs.

---

[1] Northrop Frye, in his study of Shakespeare's comedies and romances (*A Natural Perspective* [New York, 1965]) argues for the validity of a basic distinction between two classes of critics, whom he terms "Iliad critics" and "Odyssey critics." The former concern themselves with "tragedy, realism and irony," the latter with "comedy and romance." The Iliad critics (p. 2),

> "think of literature as primarily instructive, or as, in Arnold's phrase, a criticism of life. They feel that its essential function is to illuminate something about life, or reality, or experience, or whatever we call the immediate world outside literature. *They thus tend, whether they say so or not, to think of literature, taken as a whole, as a vast imaginative allegory, the end of which is a deeper understanding of the nonliterary center of experience.* They are attracted to tragedy, to realism, or to irony, because it is in these modes that they find the clearest reflection of what Freud calls the reality principle. *They value lifelike characterization, incidents close enough to actual experience to be imaginatively credible, and above all they value 'high seriousness' in theme. . . .*" (Italics mine)

The Odyssey critic, however, "simply want(s) to see what is going to happen in the story" (p. 3). Of the principles he works with perhaps the most important is that (p. 8).

> "*In comedy and romance the story seeks its own end instead of holding the mirror up to nature.* Consequently comedy and romance are so obviously conventionalized that a serious interest in them soon leads to an interest in convention itself. This shifts the center of attention from individual works of literature to the larger groupings represented by the words comedy and romance themselves and thus an interest in convention leads to an interest in genre. Then, one finds in any comedy or romance, because of the conventionalization, a number of motifs or devices that one finds in other similar stories, and so an interest in genre develops an interest in the technique of constructing stories." (Italics mine)

Now it appears that these opposing critical tendencies were already present in ancient literary theory. They correspond, in fact, fairly closely to those traditions of literary thought which we may call the Platonic and Aristotelian. (The paradigmatic work of the latter tradition is, of course, the *Poetics*.) It is not always possible, to be sure, to maintain a distinction between Aristotelian and Platonic sources of ancient literary theory in an absolutely clear-cut way, since in certain important respects the two traditions, as we shall see, overlapped. It is clear, also, that the distinction, although valid in general, needs qualification in one other respect. The category of genre criticism, what Northrop Frye calls "Odyssey criticism," does appear to the wider view to possess a kind of uniformity. Yet, as regards the other, "outer-directed" mode (Frye's "Iliad criticism"), it is evident that although the varying perspectives within it are united by the single fact that critics of this persuasion will, as a matter of general tendency, measure a work of literature against some external, non-literary reality, it is nonetheless true that they regularly do so in one of two distinct ways—modes of criticism I shall call the allegorical and the rhetorical or, alternatively, the epistemological and the ethical.[2] For there is a difference, and a very important one, when a critic sets out to measure a work of literature against external reality, between his asking whether a given work represents this external reality *truly*[3] or whether, on the other hand, the actions represented are, to his own mind, *ethically acceptable or not*. It is true that in some philosophical systems, the True and the Good are ultimately identified, but this is not inevitably the case. It may, in fact, be argued that in the common sense view good and evil are thought to enjoy an equal degree of reality. The consequences of this difference of perspective affect a sufficiently large number of critical procedures that it seems reasonable to argue that a *threefold*

---

[2] Frye, *Anatomy of Criticism* (Princeton, 1957; repr. New York, 1965), 71-128 means something rather different by ethical criticism.

[3] 'Truly': not *truly* in the sense of *truthfully* or *in a life-like way*, but in the sense that the text is believed to point to something which *really exists*. So far as I can see, this assumption almost always operates in ancient allegorical interpretations of texts. It is seemingly never a question of verisimilitude or ideal truthfulness, as it is, for example, in Aristotle's *Poetics*. The allegorical interpreter regularly supposes that the text is a reflection of some specific external reality, whether physical, psychological or metaphysical, which he *knows*, as a believer in some system of truth, to exist indubitably.

division of the tendencies of literary criticism will be closer to the facts, at least to the facts of ancient literary theory. There were, it seems, not two, but three broad streams of literary thought in antiquity. My book will be about that kind of "outer-directed" criticism which is concerned with the *truth-status* of the objects of literary representation, what I have referred to as epistemological or allegorical criticism.

But before characterizing that tradition in a preliminary way, suggesting what I take to be its importance, and giving the reader a notion of the problems to be treated in the main body of my study, it may prove useful, for purposes of contrast, to sketch, first, the tradition of genre, or "Odyssey," criticism and, then, that of ethical criticism. I shall also outline, where pertinent, the contributions of Plato and Aristotle to the formation of both of these, as well as of the allegorical, traditions, since it is clear that in literary criticism, as in so much else, the views of these two thinkers were near to all-determining for subsequent antiquity. In Plato's *Republic* (II.376E-379A), there is in fact a discussion of literature in which there already discernibly emerges, although in a not fully developed form and from a specifically Platonic perspective, those same three ways of looking at a work of literature which I have just been discussing. Plato speaks in this passage first, of the *content of stories as such* (logoi, 376E and 378A); secondly, of the *imprint* (typos, 377B) which such stories leave on the character of the listeners, as well as of the implicit *ethical sense* (also typos, 379A) in the work itself; thirdly, of the *reality which is to be found in the "undersense"* (hyponoia, 378D) or "real meaning" lying beneath the surface of the text. In these categories—story as such, implicit ethical sense, and the real and always, to the interpreter, true sense beneath the narrative façade—there is a clear prefiguration of those three streams of ancient literary criticism which make up the subject of the following discussion.

2. GENRE CRITICISM

The genre critic, and we refer above all to the Aristotle of the *Poetics*, is one who sees in the story or plot *as such* the central fact of a literary work. Plato, as we noted, also spoke of stories as such. But Plato's primary concern was with whether they were true or false, good or bad. What was of interest to Aristotle were the structures of tragic plots—their shape and direction, the mechanisms by which they were made to unfold, the kinds of characters which rendered tragic action credible and effective. Moreover, the extent of their effectiveness was not to be measured by any external standard of truthfulness or morality, but by the degree to which they contributed to realizing what Aristotle took to be the special function (*ergon*) of tragedy, the "effecting, by means of pity and fear, of the catharsis of emotions of a similar nature" (*Poetics* 6.1449a 27-28). A critical use of the notion of function was not a gratuitous imposition on Aristotle's part, for although he did obviously employ certain *a priori* notions, such as 'end,' 'nature,' as well as 'function,' he seems to have arrived at his conception of the proper function of tragedy in a largely empirical way, that is, by actually viewing and reading a large number of tragedies and by observing which ones were, in his own view or by some sort of universal judgment, the most effective. He then determined what precisely the source of this effect was. It was only at this point, I believe, that he formulated the function of tragedy—that special result which it alone, or preeminently, among the literary genres was able to achieve. As a last step he isolated those specific plot-structures which were most frequently present in effective and successful plays. The important thing about a critic like Aristotle is that literary judgments of individual plays are characteristically determined by the internal needs of the genre to which they belong. The critic will not ask whether the elements of the story reflect external reality truly or are morally acceptable, but whether they are probable or necessary in terms of tragedy's own special kinds of structure, i.e. whether they will contribute to realizing the function of tragedy. And so, when Aristotle does consider whether a character is good or bad, he does not do so with an eye on external standards of moral judgment, but only in order to determine whether a character is situated on precisely that point on the moral scale where he will best aid the achievement of the function of the genre.[4] For a critic like Aristotle, as we see him in the *Poetics*, it is above all in terms of the inherent requirements of a work of literature, and of the genre to which it belongs, that one poses ethical or epistemological questions. Neither morality nor truthfulness in themselves can provide the

---

[4] 'Realizing the function of tragedy': see especially ch. 25 of the *Poetics*. 'Achievement of the function of the genre': see ch. 13, especially 1452b28-1453a12.

critic with self-sufficient means for judgment. Literature is not held up to life, but instead to its own implicit, perfect form.

This view of what constitutes the chief basis of literary judgment was in the ancient as in the modern world rather in the minority. It appears, indeed, that it was only those critics who were self-consciously in the Aristotelian tradition, such as the great Alexandrian scholar, Aristarchus of Samothrace, who worked with the same critical assumptions. Aristarchus' critical work on Homer is now lost, but enough survives, for the most part in the attenuated form of marginal notes in medieval manuscripts of Homer, that we are able to perceive the outline of his critical thought. Let us cite one example. The recognition of Odysseus by his dog Argos after twenty years, and the sudden death of the dog exactly where he lay, struck some ancient critics as improbable. Aristarchus' answer, it seems, was that the details of this episode were devised *for the sake of the plot*. The dog recognized its master in the way that it did *in order that* Eumaeus could think that it was he, and not Odysseus, who was being greeted. The disguise of Odysseus could remain undetected, because the dog died immediately upon recognizing him, without going up to his master, and could therefore exhibit no compromising signs of affection. As with Aristotle, it is the shape and general needs of the plot which determine individual details.[5]

3. ETHICAL CRITICISM

In those forms of criticism in which a literary work is measured against external reality, there have been two recurrent and distinct questions. First, "Does the content of the work represent some external reality which truly exists?" Then, "Are the ethical standards implicit in the details of the work acceptable and worthy of emulation?" The difference between the two, however, is not merely that between two practically distinct areas of critical study. The difference also involves consequences for the way in which the critic conceives of fundamental literary processes, such as, among others, the relationship between copy and model, i.e.

---

[5] For further details, see Ad. Roemer, *Die Homerexegese Aristarchs* (Paderborn, 1924), 69-71. We are reminded of the critical position implicit in Frye's observation on Blifil in *Tom Jones*: "If one starts to tell a story about Tom Jones, one needs such a character as Blifil for structural reasons, not merely to symbolize the author's disapproval of hypocrisy" (*A Natural Perspective*, p. 40).

the process of mimesis, and the degree of conscious intention to be attributed to the artist.

One may characterize the ethical critics, in a preliminary way, as in general less philosophical in their approach to criticism than the allegorical critics. The canons of ethical judgment brought to bear by rhetorical critics like Dionysius of Halicarnassus were usually more or less universally accepted notions of ethical behavior. Rather than the doctrines of some particular philosophical school, such critics tended to incorporate into their critical systems the views of their own broadly educated class. The norms of conduct, moreover, which served as models were not usually conceived of, as they were by some philosophers, as enjoying a separate, transcendent existence. They were instead habitually perceived in, and seen as inseparable from, the concrete reality of words and actions, the various ways in which people, in and out of books, talked and behaved. From this perspective, criticism tended to become a preoccupation with style viewed as the *characteristic* manner of speaking of an author or his characters, and with paradigmatic acts—in other words, with those gestures, whether verbal or actional, by which a habitual cast of mind is realized with special and exemplary clarity. Thus, it was with the implications of behavior (and I consider style as a form of behavior) rather than, as in allegorical criticism, with a set of preexisting conceptions or abiding natural realities that the rhetorical critic was concerned.

That ancient critics were aware of the difference between these two crititical perspectives is clear from a passage in an essay of Plutarch; he is discussing the Song of Ares and Aphrodite from the eighth book of Homer's *Odyssey*:

> "Now these declarations and opinions contained in the words of the text [6] may be discovered by anybody who will pay the attention, but *from the actions themselves the poets supply other lessons*; ... [However], *By forcibly distorting these stories through what used to be termed 'deeper meanings' (hyponoiai) but are nowadays called 'allegorical interpretations,'* some persons say that the sun is represented as giving information about Aphrodite in the arms of Ares, because the conjunction of the planet Mars with Venus portends births conceived in adultery, and when the sun returns in its course and discovers these, they cannot be kept secret.... *as though the*

---

[6] Plutarch is referring to passages where some point of view, ethical or other, finds explicit expression.

poet himself did not afford the right solutions. For, in the account of Aphrodite, he teaches those who will pay attention that vulgar music, coarse songs, and stories treating of vile themes, create licentious characters, unmanly lives, and men that love luxury, soft living, intimacy with women and
> *Changes of clothes, warm baths, and the genial bed of enjoyment."*
(Odyssey 8.239)[7]

Absorbing social values from concrete example, whether in one's own experience, or in the reading of the canonical books of one's culture is, of course, a mode of socialization universal in human history. It is precisely, in fact, that form of moral instruction which Plato aims to discredit again and again in his dialogues; in these, Socrates and a philosophically naive interlocutor are repeatedly portrayed as running up against contradictions which arise from an effort to define some moral category in terms of concrete actions rather than abstract definitions free of internal contradiction. Plutarch, however, despite the fact of Platonic influence, was in matters of ethics much more a man of average sensibility, and his views may be taken as representative.

In theory, both style and content are the legitimate objects of critical examination, but ethical criticism, generally speaking, is most fruitfully studied in those critics who were chiefly students of style. Not that the actions portrayed in literary works were not subjected to ethical judgment. The essay of Plutarch just cited, as well as many other critical works and isolated passages of literary comment, bear witness to this kind of literary judgment. We may recall, for example, the passage in the treatise on Thucydides by the Augustan critic, Dionysius of Halicarnassus, in which Herodotus is deemed a 'more sensible' author than Thucydides, because he portrayed actions, i.e. the Greek resistance to the Persians, which were morally more praiseworthy than much of what Thucydides relates about the Peloponnesian War.[8] Nonetheless, it is true that in the ancient world the important achievement of an ethically colored mode of criticism lay in the analysis of the way an author spoke, or had his characters speak, in other words, in what we usually call rhetorical or stylistic criticism.[9]

---

[7] *How the Young Man Should Study Poetry* (19E-20A), tr. Babbit (Cambridge, Mass., Loeb Library, 1927 and reprints). The italics in the text are my own.

[8] Dionysius of Halicarnassus, *Epistula ad Pompeium*, 3.2-6, in *Opuscula*, vol. 2, ed. Usener & Radermacher.

[9] The following books are good introductions: C. S. Baldwin, *Ancient*

Now it was above all Aristotle who, in the third book of his *Rhetoric*, established the structures and methods of this tradition of criticism, although it is fairly clear that in this matter his achievement was less original than was the case with genre criticism. For it seems that what Aristotle did was to incorporate into his theory of stylistic analysis—in many of its particular insights, without doubt, quite original—a conception of style already well established in classical thought, according to which the manner in which an author wrote was viewed as an analogue to the way people behaved in general. The fact that in his *Rhetoric* Aristotle should have started with premises reflecting such a widely held view is not at all surprising, when we recall the fact that he followed very much the same procedure in other "practical" works, such as the *Ethics* or *Politics*.

Before Aristotle we find these same assumptions operating in critical scrutinies of literary works. In Aristophanes' *Frogs*, to take one instance, Euripides is repeatedly castigated for the low moral level of the characters whose actions he portrays. But he is also attacked for the immoral implications of his *style*, an immorality which, in Aristophanes' analysis, finds one of its clearest manifestations in the anarchic character of Euripidean lyric. For there is, as has been pointed out, good reason for assuming a connection between Aristophanes' parody of Euripidean monody, in which it is above all the quality of structural and semantic dissolution which is emphasized, and his portrayal of the underworld visited by Dionysus as an infernal, yet in some way true, vision of Aristophanes' own society.[10] For in that vision what stands out above all else is the complete inversion of established social values and classes. It is mob rule in Hades, with Euripides at the head:

Rhetoric and Poetic (New York, 1924); S. F. Bonner, *The Literary Treatises of Dionysius of Halicarnassus* (Cambridge, 1939; repr. 1969); D. L. Clark, *Rhetoric in Greco-Roman Education* (New York, 1957); George Kennedy, *The Art of Persuasion in Greece* (Princeton, 1963); George Kennedy, *The Art of Rhetoric in the Roman World* (Princeton, 1972); G. M. A. Grube, *The Greek and Roman Critics* (London, 1965); Heinrich Lausberg, *Handbuch der literarischen Rhetorik*, 2 vols. (Munich, 1960); R. L. Volkmann, *Die Rhetorik der Griechen und Römer* [2] (Leipzig, 1874).

[10] *Frogs* 1309-1363. For a good discussion of these points, see Ch. Segal, 'The Character of Dionysus and the Unity of the Frogs,' *Harvard Studies in Classical Philology* 65 (1961) 207-242, esp. 212-217.

"A great, great contest has been set into motion
among the dead, and there is much civil strife.

. . . .

When Euripides descended, he began to show off his skill
to the footpads and the purse-snatchers,
the patricides and burglars-precisely those
who make up the majority in Hades. They gave ear
to his counter-arguments, his twistings and turnings.
They became completely mad about him and thought him the
cleverest man.
Heartened, he took hold of the throne where, before, Aeschylus
had been."

(*Frogs* 759-760, 771-778)

Very much the same critical point of view is implicit in Socrates'
examination of the nature and effects of literature which occupies
Books II and III of the *Republic*. I limit my present remarks to
these books, for although some of the arguments foreshadow the
positions of Book X, they are nonetheless primarily written with
an eye to the problems of *pre-philosophical* education, and necessarily so, since the training of the philosopher is introduced only
in Book V. At the level of cognition of the non-philosophical
guardians of II and III, the perception of truth, i.e. of the Forms,
is necessarily excluded; the guardians move in the world of opinion
only. For Plato the epistemological category of opinion found its
literary manifestation in both the *notions* of morality which are
implied by the narrative or dramatic details of a literary work and
in the concrete *actions*, whether true or false, which are represented
by the poet. And like opinion in general these literary "opinions"
could be right or wrong, true or false. Like extra-literary opinion,
too, they were assimilated directly without supporting argument,
i.e. non-dialectically and as part of the sensuous experience of
literature. It should be made clear, however, that in contrast to
Book X, the emphasis here is on the moral effects of experiencing
"false stories" (for example, those about the gods) and not primarily,
if at all, on the ontological remoteness from ideal truth of all
literary representations, whether true or false.[11]

---

[11] A brief reminder of the Platonic epistemology assumed in these discussions of poetry. Where there is no direct dialectical *proof* of the truth of a
statement, there can only be *opinion*. A statement may, of course, be true;
but where philosophical proof is lacking, one can speak only, at best, of
true opinion. Likewise, where belief is false, and of necessity unsupportable
by dialectic, there is *false opinion*. Despite the opposition of true and false,

In this portion of the *Republic*, Plato's literary ideas are very close to what we have characterized as the mainstream conception of the ethical critics, and it is here that the contrast with Aristotle, at least the Aristotle of the *Rhetoric*, is the least sharp. To be sure, the values and the truths which Plato would like to see implicit in works of literature are those not of every man, but of the philosopher. However, the conception of literature chiefly as a vehicle for paradigmatic words and acts is fundamentally the same. Plato, too, saw such behavior both in actions portrayed and in the way in which the author or character speaks:

> " 'Nor can we permit stories of wars and plots and battles among the gods; they are quite untrue, and if we want our prospective guardians to believe that quarrelsomeness is one of the worst of evils, we must certainly not let them embroider robes with the story of the Battle of the Giants, or tell them the tales about the many and various quarrels between gods and heroes and their friends and relations. On the contrary, if we are to persuade them that no citizen has ever quarrelled with any other, because it is sinful, our old men and women must tell children stories with this end in view from the first, and we must compel our poets to tell them similar stories when they grow up.' " (378B-D, tr. Lee)

and

> " 'But what about the style and content of the poetry themselves?' I asked. 'Don't they depend on character, just as the other things depend on them?'
> 'They must.'
> 'Good literature, therefore, and good music and beauty of form generally all depend on goodness of character; I don't mean that lack of awareness of the world which we politely call "goodness," but a character of real judgement and principle.'
> 'I quite agree.'
> 'And are not these things which our young men must try to acquire, if they are to perform their function in life properly?'
> 'They must.'
> 'And they are to be seen in painting and similar arts, in weaving and embroidery, in architecture and furniture, and in living things, animals and plants. For in all of these we find beauty and ugliness. And ugliness of form and disharmony are akin to bad art and bad character, and their opposites are akin to and represent good character and discipline.'
> 'That is perfectly true.'

---

both forms of opinion stand together *below* the major break in the divided line (*Republic* 509D-511E); both are *philosophically* without ultimate value.

'It is not only to the poets therefore that we must issue orders requiring them to represent good character in their poems or not to write at all; we must issue similar orders to all artists and prevent them portraying bad character, ill-discipline, meanness, or ugliness in painting, sculpture, architecture, or any work of art, and if they are unable to comply they must be forbidden to practise their art. We shall thus prevent our guardians being brought up among representations of what is evil, and so day by day and little by little, by feeding as it were in an unhealthy pasture, insensibly doing themselves grave psychological damage.' "

(400D-401C) [12]

In the latter passage there is a particularly clear expression of the double perspective which was to remain characteristic of ethical criticism—the belief, on the one hand, that a work of literature was a revelation of character and that, on the other, the reader is as deeply influenced by exposure to varying kinds of literary behavior, among these stylistic behavior, as he is by that of human beings in ordinary, non-literary contexts. For Plato, of course, ethical criticism of literature represents a philosophical compromise; it is pertinent only when one is concerned with non-philosophical instruction. The position of Books II-III is thus very much an "ironic" position, the product of a "realistic" Plato attempting to do the best that can be done in the context of a practically realizable society and offering a program to which he gives only qualified assent. As in the *Phaedrus*, there is the implication that, among philosophers, the effect or status of a literary work is a question of no ultimate importance. Despite the fact, however, that Plato did address himself to these problems, even if from his own qualified perspective, it remains true that it was chiefly Aristotle's *Rhetoric* which determined the methods and premises of ancient ethical criticism in that form of stylistic or rhetorical criticism in which it achieved its greatest successes.

The decisiveness of Aristotle's influence on subsequent rhetorical theory and, in particular, the importance of his discussion of style in chapters 1-12 of Book III are facts generally accepted by scholars and require no special demonstration. To be sure, there is reason to believe that the *Rhetoric*, like Aristotle's other systematic works, was not widely known outside of Peripatetic circles until the middle of the first century B.C. Nevertheless, the treatise of Aristotle's pupil, Theophrastus, *On Style*, which, so far as we can

---

[12] Plato, *The Republic*, tr. H. D. P. Lee (Baltimore, 1955).

reconstruct it, clearly depended on the Third Book of the *Rhetoric* for its stylistic categories, evidently exerted a great influence on the rhetorical theory of the Hellenistic period. This is not to say that Hellenistic and Roman rhetoric were not without innovations— one might cite the contributions of Hermagoras to the theory of proofs—and rhetorical theory at the hands of critics like Cicero, Quintilian, and "Longinus" was significantly refashioned to meet changing social and political conditions or to satisfy new spiritual aspirations. It is also true that the contribution of pre-Aristotelian rhetoricians should not be underestimated. Nonetheless the outline of rhetoric which Aristotle proposed and the various stylistic categories and techniques of analysis which he and his pupil, Theophrastus, elaborated were the major foundation of rhetoric and the study of style in the ancient world. Their influence is to be discerned in numerous details in the works of Demetrius, Cicero, Dionysius of Halicarnassus and "Longinus." [13]

The reasons for this are doubtless many, but the one that is especially pertinent, because of the ethical perspective from which literature was customarily viewed by the rhetorical critics, was the fact that Aristotle's own theory of style was based, in a clear way, on ethical notions similar to those he enunciates in his *Ethics*, and, further, that these same ethical notions correspond closely to those we have already argued are implicit in the stylistic judgments of the rhetorical critics. I mean by this that Aristotle in his *Ethics* saw behavioral norms, and in this he reflected the views of his fellow Greeks, as something chiefly implicit in actual behavior, as not enjoying some separate prior existence and as thus actualizable only in repeated, habitual actions. Therefore, when Aristotle came to discuss style, clearly in his eyes, too, a form of behavior, he was able, with the power of a great systematizing intellect, to make explicit in this context precisely those unstated assumptions regarding the relationship between style and behavior in general which formed the basis of an ethical judgement of literature. In reading the *Rhetoric* one cannot help but be struck by the importance of concepts which are clearly derived from Aristotle's ethical thought. For one thing, there is the doctrine of the Mean which Aristotle uses in his definition of

---

[13] See especially, Friedrich Solmsen, 'The Aristotelian Tradition in Ancient Rhetoric,' *American Journal of Philology* 62 (1941) 42-50 and 169-190. Johannes Stroux, *De Theophrasti Virtutibus Dicendi* (Leipzig, 1912).

the one essential 'virtue' of style, clarity (*sapheneia*). If the only consideration were Aristotle's use of the word 'virtue' in this context, one might discount the influence of his ethical thought, since the word may already have been used as a critical term before Aristotle wrote the undoubtedly late third book of the *Rhetoric*.[14] The fact, however, that Aristotle analyzed the central stylistic virtue of his system in terms of the fundamentally important concept of the Mean, and his ways of talking about style in general, suggest that he perceived a more than superficial connection between stylistic and ethical forms of behavior.

Aristotelian ethics was, in comparison with Plato's, distinctly *non-intellectualistic*, at least as regards the moral virtues—and it is these which we should argue are analogous to the stylistic virtues of the rhetoricians. That is, although Aristotle believes that conscious, rational reflection does affect ethical choice, it is nonetheless mainly true that the source of proper ethical choice is long habituation, or practice, in correct behavior. This is quite a different matter from Plato's philosopher, who makes ethical choices with the eye of his intellect fixed on eternal models of justice and the other virtues.[15] The consequence of this fact, if we are correct in our belief in a connection in Aristotle between ethics and style, is that style, too, was viewed by Aristotle primarily as a habitual or gestural, rather than an intellectual form of behavior. Like a man's way of walking, dressing or speaking, style will be the expression of a certain *cast of mind*, of a certain *men-*

---

[14] On the general question of the relatively late date of the third book of the *Rhetoric* (relatively, that is, to the first two books), see Friedrich Solmsen, *Die Entwicklung der aristotelischen Logik und Rhetorik* (= *Neue philologische Untersuchungen*, 4) (Berlin, 1929).

[15] See *Nichomachean Ethics*, II.1.1103a14 ff, 4.1105a26 ff. for characteristic ways of talking about ethical questions. As regards the analogy between Aristotle's moral virtues and vices and the stylistic virtues and vices of the rhetoricians, it should be noted that already in the *Rhetoric* and the *Poetics*, the term, to take one example, which Aristotle uses to designate the vicious "excess" of *clarity* (Aristotle's chief stylistic virtue) also commonly bore an ethical sense. For *tapeinos* (*Rhet*. III.2. 1404b 3, 6; *Poetics* 1458a 18, 20, 22) besides meaning 'plain' or 'lowly,' could have the morally derogatory sense 'cheap' or 'commonplace.' One further example from many will help to make the point clearer. In the rhetoricians, *megaloprepeia*, a term expressing the opposite quality to that expressed by *tapeinos*, was commonly used to denote a tone of stylistic grandeur or solemnity (Dionysius of Halicarnassus, *On Composition*, 16; idem, *Thucydides*, 23; Demetrius, *On Style*, 37). *Megaloprepeia* is, of course, one of the most strikingly treated of Aristotle's ethical virtues (*Ethics*, IV.2.1122a18-1123a19).

tality rather than a conscious medium for expressing intellectually perceived models.

We have already spoken of the fact that it seemed natural to Aristotle to transfer to a stylistic context one of the basic conceptual tools of his ethics, that is, the theory of virtue conceived of as a dynamic mean. But apart from this point of primary importance, there are other passages where the same fact is evident. In the passage in the *Rhetoric* where he defines the virtue of 'clarity' in terms of the mean, he says:

> "Words are like men; as we feel a difference between people from afar and our fellow townsmen, so it is with our feeling for language. And hence it is well to give the ordinary idiom an air of remoteness; the hearers are struck by what is out of the way, and like what strikes them." (III. 1404b 8-12, tr. Cooper)
> Or again, in speaking of propriety:
> "The speaker must find epithets and metaphors alike that are fitting. . . . Otherwise the impropriety will be glaring. . . . Instead, we must search thus: a crimson cloak befits a young man; what dress befits an old one? The same clothing is not appropriate to both."
> (III. 1405a 10-14) [16]

The belief that "words are like men," or that canons of propriety can be applied to style in the same way that they can to a man's dress, is indeed at the very heart of ethical criticism. *Le style c'est l'homme même.* This assumption is universally present in the ancient rhetorical critics, and can be illustrated with special clarity in "Longinus"; in speaking of the stylistic virtue of sublimity, the author says:

> "Sublimity is the echo of a great spirit. . . . First, it is absolutely necessary to establish the source of this quality, namely, that the true writer must have no thoughts which are mean or ignoble. For it is impossible for those who think petty and slavish thoughts the whole of their lives to produce anything worthy of admiration and deserving to live for all time. For their words are great, as you would expect, whose minds are full and weighty."
> (*On the Sublime,* 9.2-3)

The first step toward a clear distinction between the two forms of "Iliad criticism" has, I hope, been made. In the one view, that of ethical criticism, intention or meaning, some prior intelligible

---

[16] *The Rhetoric of Aristotle*, tr. Lane Cooper (New York, 1932). "Words are like men" is not a literal rendering of Aristotle's Greek, but it brings out the implied sense very well.

model, are not divorced from surface and afforded a separate status. In rhetorical or stylistic analysis, one does not properly ask, "What does this writer *mean*?" Rather, "What is a man who writes this way *like*?" or "Is this way of writing *appropriate* to such and such a kind of man?" In the allegorical mode of criticism, on the other hand, as we shall presently see, the interpreter will characteristically ask, "What does our author *intend* when he writes this way?" In a word, the allegorical method is marked by a search for *intention*; the other, ethical criticism, by an effort at *characterization*.

In this critical attention to characterization a central, controlling notion is that of *propriety*. As Aristotle says, some metaphors are as inappropriate to certain contexts as a crimson cloak is to an old man. Propriety presupposes, of course, a more or less unchallenged and stable system of values and social categories. It is only when most men agree as to what is proper and what is not, and what constitutes the "natural" attributes of a certain class, sex or age group that the notion of propriety can have much force. It is therefore not surprising that in rhetorical criticism, in view of its normative ethical views, appropriateness became a fundamentally important literary concept. Propriety is that tool which will regularly be brought to bear when the critic must decide whether an author is "behaving," or is having his characters "behave" as they ought to—as they ought to, of course, according to the critic's own ethical and social preconceptions. Stated from a different angle, if a writer employs a style marked by certain characteristics, the critic will assume that, since such characteristics are suitable to a given character in terms of universally recognized canons of propriety, then the writer, or his creations, must be of such a character. In a word, it is by his stylistic behavior that a writer is habitually judged.

4. ALLEGORICAL CRITICISM

The allegorical critic, on the other hand, is typically the representative of a sectarian point of view, the advocate of some religion or philosophical school. He may be Jew or Christian, Stoic or Neoplatonist, but in his view a work of literature is significant above all because it contains representations of what he takes to be certain and irrefutable truth about the nature of reality, whether physical, psychological, divine or metaphysical. In such a critical milieu, propriety, with its clear dependence on universally accepted norms of correctness, will obviously not figure significantly. In its place we find a concern with conscious *purpose* or *intention*, these being perceived generally as specific religious or philosophical doctrines residing in the mind of the author which it is his conscious aim to represent through concrete narrative for the reader's enlightenment. It is not surprising therefore that allegorical criticism flourished chiefly among critics who were of a more philosophical bent than was generally the case with the rhetorical critics. Such an approach to literary interpretation necessarily presupposed some sort of serious interest in abstract thought on the part of the interpreter, since the uncovering of such thought in a text was the announced goal of the allegorical critic.

So overriding a concern with ideas which were assumed to preexist the text in which they were discerned had a variety of consequences with respect both to methods of interpretation and to the intellectual attitudes of critics who were drawn to this mode of exegesis. As regards the latter point, one may say, with only some degree of simplification, that there were two leading philosophical prejudices which tended to predispose to allegorical thinking. The one was the belief in an unseen order of being which, in its greater degree of reality, was viewed as the cause or model of "our" world, the world of the senses, a view preeminently exemplified, of course, by Platonism. The other predisposing factor was the belief that behind the working of the universe there lay some kind of conscious *purpose*. In this view, argued along familiar teleological lines, everything in the universe was the product of a conscious, designing intellect, which strove, as best it was able,[17] to ensure that every element of that universe served the best possible end. As regards the Neoplatonists, it need scarcely be pointed out that they were thinkers for whom both of these philosophical assumptions were of central importance.

Now, in the context of such philosophical beliefs, a work of literature will almost necessarily come to be viewed in a number of specific ways. We have already spoken of a critical concern on the part of the allegorist with the author's intention. Viewed in the light of the leading philosophical ideas just considered, this will mean that the critic's habit of thought is to see the text as existing

---

[17] For this point, cf. *Timaeus* 30B with Cornford's discussion, *Plato's Cosmology* (London, 1937), 35-37.

on two distinct levels: first, the level of ideas which reside in the
author's mind, his intention, and, then, the level of concrete
narrative details, these two levels corresponding, in the wider
scheme, to the world of intelligible reality and that of phenomenal
experience. It also means that the critic will regularly assume that
every narrative feature can be viewed as, in principle, the product
of conscious design on the part of the writer and as therefore
susceptible to, in fact demanding, intentional analysis. From such
a perspective a literary text does not have the exemplary function
it had for the ethical critics, nor does it exhibit that union of form
and content which was assumed by the genre critic. Instead, it
was seen as a shadow cast by some more abundant reality, a veil
before a mystery which one is invited to lift aside, a riddle which
calls for an answer from those whose special knowledge gives
them the means to provide a solution.

In the context of such thought, two critical questions came to
assume particular importance. First, do the surface details of a
text under examination represent something which is abidingly,
that is, philosophically, true? Or are they pure fictions, shadows,
as it were, without a source, diverting enough, but with no sub-
stratum of reality to nourish them. Plato's false stories of Books
II and III of the *Republic* are of such a nature, even though the
metaphysical apparatus had not yet been worked out at that
point in the dialogue which could illuminate their deficiency in the
fullest way. Moreover, as we saw, Plato's emphasis was rather on
the moral consequences of their falsity than on their impoverished
ontological status.

There is a second question—one which concerned the Platonist
allegorist above all—and this arose from the doubts which Plato
expressed in the 10th Book of the *Republic* about the very *possibility* of literature representing anything but phenomenal reality.
Clearly such an assertion, if accepted as categorically true, would
have discredited allegorical interpretation as a mode of literary
criticism. In the first place, however, Plato's own stand on this
matter, when viewed in the context of his whole work, was, I
believe, marked by certain ambiguities. And it was precisely these
ambiguities, we shall argue in the next chapter, which made a
reconciliation with Plato possible for the Neoplatonists. Nonetheless, the Neoplatonists, as we know from Proclus and other sources,
were seriously troubled by Plato's objections, because they cor-

rectly perceived the consequences they entailed for their own
exegetical assumptions. But by, among other things, exploiting
Plato's own ambiguities, they were able to offer answers to these
objections, and these answers, impressive in themselves and
important for the course of the history of literary theory, will be
the subject of this study. There was another aspect of Plato's
rejection of the value of literary representation to which the
Neoplatonists also addressed themselves, and this was his belief
that in mirroring the lowest level of reality, representation had
necessarily harmful effects on the souls of those who were exposed
to literature, because it nourished precisely those parts of the
soul whose growth weakened the power of reason to perceive
the world of Forms.

Apart from the self-evident value of putting in a somewhat
clearer light an episode in the history of thought which has not
yet been treated in a sufficiently systematic and available way,
there are several other reasons why an investigation of the history
of ancient allegorism is not without relevance. First is the fact that
modern histories of ancient literary criticism and theory, for
whatever reasons, generally exhibit an anti-allegorical bias. And
even when this bias is seemingly absent, the effect is very much the
same, since such histories are written as if the rhetorical tradition,
and the less wide-spread tradition of genre criticism, were the
only modes of literary interpretation in the ancient world with a
respectable claim to the attention of modern students of literature.
This assumption is, I believe, historically and intellectually un-
justified. For one thing, it is clear that the attitudes of historians
of ancient literary theory, now and at other times, are only a
particular expression of prevailing critical prejudices, and in this
matter it seems to be a fact that much of the critical thought of the
last century or so has been marked by an anti-allegorical bias.
However, the claims of this intellectual fashion, like most others,
precisely because it is in large part the product of special historical
conditions, can themselves be put in a more accurate perspective by
certain historical considerations. One may point out that until the
nineteenth century allegorical criticism has been a central and per-
sistent element of literary thought.[18] More relevantly to our study,

---

[18] See the useful discussion of Angus Fletcher, with excellent bibliography,
in his article 'Allegory,' *Dictionary of the History of Ideas*, vol. i, ed. Ph.
Wiener (New York, 1968) 41-48.

allegorical techniques were consistently used in the Greek world from about 500 B.C. on in the elucidation of texts by interpreters of the most disparate religious and philosophical persuasions. These interpreters were often men of considerable intellectual eminence, and there seems little point, and not much fairness either, in blinding oneself to the fact that they were asking serious and important questions about the meaning of the texts to which they and others since have devoted so much study. And if they did so from philosophical and methodological premises which seem suspect in the light of modern preconceptions, we should nonetheless try to give the claims of the allegorists an impartial hearing.

It is not only that much of the neglect of the allegorical tradition on the part of historians of criticism can be attributed to intellectual parochialism, and that such parochialism has disseminated historical stereotypes which require correction. There is an additional relevance which lies in the fact that many practicing critics are themselves "covert" allegorists. Frye has put the case very clearly:

> "In fact, all commentary, or the relating of the events of narrative to conceptual terminology, is in one sense allegorical interpretation. To say that *Hamlet* is a tragedy of indecision is to start setting up beside *Hamlet* the kind of moral counterpart to its events that an allegory has as part of its structure. Whole libraries of criticism may be written on the fictions of *Hamlet* or *Macbeth*, bringing out aspects of their meaning that would not occur to other readers, and all such commentary might be said, by a ready extension of the term, to allegorize the plays." [19]

If this is true, and I think it is, there is some value in studying a tradition of criticism in which allegorical assumptions are stated explicitly and the interpretative problems which such assumptions entail are faced openly and not, as is the case with "covert" allegorism, left unexamined and unresolved.[20]

The present study, then, is an examination in detail of a chapter in the history of allegorism which has up to now been relatively neglected. The reasons for this neglect—and we must keep in mind those general ones I have already outlined—are that the specific texts I shall be studying, the Neoplatonic commentaries on

---

[19] *The Princeton Encyclopedia of Poetry and Poetics*, ed. A. Preminger, *s.v.* 'Allegory' (Princeton, 1965), 12-13.

[20] One thinks of the ease with which many critics beg the question of intention by reference to the "unconscious intention" of a writer.

Plato's dialogues, have apparently been thought to possess little relevance or value by those historians of criticism for whom figures like Longinus, Horace or Aristotle represent the unquestioned norm. Historians of philosophy, on the other hand, who are generally those who have edited the commentaries and devoted their scholarly efforts to their elucidation, have been led to study them chiefly from the perspective of their own interest in problems of the philosophy of the late ancient world. Thus, although some excellent scholarly work has been done on techniques of interpretation in the Neoplatonic commentaries, this has almost never been related to the wider context of ancient literary thought. The result is that the Neoplatonic commentaries have very largely fallen between two scholarly stools. As a consequence, a significant episode in the history of literary thought has gone largely unwritten.

As I mentioned, the texts whose leading exegetical ideas will be examined are the dozen or so surviving commentaries on Platonic dialogues written by Neoplatonic philosophers of the 5th and 6th centuries A.D. in Athens and Alexandria. Chief among these philosophers was the scholarch of the 5th century Academy, Proclus. The commentaries have come down to us in varying states; some whole, some fragmentary, one (Proclus on the *Cratylus*) extant only in an excerpted version. The form, or layout, of the commentaries differs, too; some follow the lemma-form, i.e. the commentary is a running, line-by-line discussion of Plato's text, which is divided for purposes of interpretation into small units, at times consisting of only a few words. On the other hand, Proclus' commentary on the *Republic* is made up of monographic treatments of whole portions of the dialogue, and in these essays there is abandoned, at least in part, the procedure of line-by-line comment.

The Neoplatonic commentaries on Plato had one explicit aim, that of clarifying Plato's philosophical intentions. This is true, even if, from a present-day perspective, the real aim seems to have been just as often that of demonstrating that Plato was a Neoplatonist before his time. In the course of their observations, the commentators at times took the pains to enunciate—we should keep in mind that they were, if anything, systematic thinkers—the exegetical principles which formed the basis of their interpretations. As their statements make clear the Neoplatonists commentators were the heirs of a tradition which was by their time of a decidedly eclectic character. A major part in this tradition was, of course, the body of arguments and perceptions concerning literary and aesthetic matters which make up an important part of the Platonic corpus. As well, there was the wider tradition of allegorical exegesis which by the time of Proclus had been practiced for already close to a thousand years in the Greek-speaking world. The history of this tradition is only fragmentarily known, but what remains gives a sufficiently vivid conception of its character, variety and achievements. Its influence on non-Greek religious movements of the time, such as Judaism and Christianity, was, as we know, considerable.

Indeed, because of the indisputable importance of the tradition of the allegorical reading of texts, a short historical survey is necessary at this point. In this the emphasis will be on allegory in the sense of *allegorism* or *allegorization* (German *Allegorese*), i.e. the systematic interpretation of a text (usually of considerable length) on the assumption that the author *intended* that the reader seek beneath the surface some second or indirect meaning, or meanings, which, in the view of the interpreter, can be related to the apparent or direct meaning in a fairly systematic way. Allegory in this sense differs, if not ultimately in structure, at least in extent, from the *figure* allegory as this was understood by the rhetoricians. The basic similarity exists for rhetorician and allegorical interpreter alike that surface and other meanings are seen to be somehow at variance, but there does seem to be a genuine difference between the two in the fact that the rhetoricians, for the most part, concerned themselves with *figures*, which are generally of limited compass—allegorical "passages," not entire works. More importantly, the emphasis with the rhetoricians was characteristically on the art of *writing*, and their discussions of figures used by the classical poets and prose writers almost always had the aim, whether stated or not, of providing examples for literary imitation. In the case of the allegorists, however, the primary concern is the elucidation of the meaning concealed beneath the surface of what often came to be viewed as virtually a sacred text. With the allegorists, literary instruction, *per se*, played no role. (For a discussion of some aspects of allegory as a rhetorical figure, see Appendix II of Chapter 2). What the following brief survey will be concerned with, then, is not the rhetoricians' theory of allegory, but allegorical interpretation by the adherents of certain philosophical and religious movements in the ancient world.

Allegorization began early in Greece (the end of the 6th century B.C.) and arose, seemingly from the beginning, out of two distinct, but complementary motives. For along with the wish to rescue the ancient poets from the charge of moral baseness and defamation of the gods, a charge which became more and more insistent in the fifth and fourth centuries (e.g. Xenophanes and Plato), there was the understandable impulse to exploit the sanctity of certain ancient texts for the purpose of furthering philosophical or religious views to which the interpreter was personally committed. This was done—and here we meet an important constant in the history of allegorical interpretation—by systematically reading into the text under scrutiny precisely those doctrines which the interpreter, in his partisan way, believed to have been anticipated in some remotely distant past and enshrined in texts which he and his contemporaries had come to view with profound reverence. 'Defensive' and 'positive' allegory thus worked hand in hand from the outset, and necessarily so, since the partisan interpreter could not promote his own views by this strategy without also insisting on the sacred and infallible character of the text under examination. At any rate, there is evidence that at least one major philosophical school of the fifth century, the Anaxagoreans, read Homer in such a way as to find in his words clear "anticipation," and thus indisputable "confirmation," of their own physical doctrines. Such modes of exegesis came under attack quite early, and already in Plato we find a serious critique of the allegorical method. It is important to note, however, that Plato nowhere clearly rejects allegorization *per se*, but only its improper use. He seems, indeed, on balance to have had something of a stimulating effect on subsequent allegorists, for by subjecting Homeric and Hesiodic theology to so thoroughgoing a critique he made even more necessary the systematic development and use of allegorical exegesis, and by challenging the use of allegory in certain contexts he forced the allegorists to formulate, out of a defensive need, more carefully thought-out theoretical positions about the nature and use of allegorical interpretation. It should also be pointed out that, besides affording such unintended stimuli, Plato, a pervasive influence in post-Classical antiquity, paradoxically fostered allegorism in another way, in that his philosophy can plausibly be characterized as an inherently 'pro-allegorical' view of the world. For in the eyes of both Platonist and allegorist—this is especially

true of the pagan allegorist—truth is something which lies hidden
behind and separate from the visible surface of things. Whether
they were affected or not by the specific impetus of Plato's thought,
it is an historical fact that certain later religious and philosophical
movements adopted allegory as an integral part of their speculative
activities. There were, however, four great sects of which this was
especially true, Stoicism, Judaism, Christianity and Neoplatonism,
and it is to some brief remarks on these that we now turn.

In the centuries which immediately followed on the conquests of
Alexander the Great, Stoicism, more than any other school, sus-
tained and forwarded the cause of allegorism. The methods of the
Stoic exegetes is probably best exemplified in the Homeric com-
mentaries of the Pergamene scholar, Crates of Mallos (2nd century
B.C.). His views regarding the interpretation of early Greek poetry
differed in virtually every important respect from those of the
Alexandrian scholars, especially Aristarchus, whose critical doctrines have already been briefly discussed. For Crates, as for the
Stoics in general, Homer, Hesiod and the other poets of early
Greece were privy to the truth about human, natural and divine
matters at a time in human life when this truth was, somehow,
less distorted and obscured than it was in the time in which the
Stoics themselves lived. Through the medium of epic poetry, in a
way that was both appropriate to the grandeur of the subject and
designed to keep hidden from the profane these most sacred teach-
ings, Homer and his fellow-poets left for posterity, at least that
part of posterity which was skilled in the allegorists' art, a complete
exposition of the deepest philosophical truths. For the Stoics the
ancient poems were like mysteries, and their true sense was covered
by the veil which was made up by the surface events of the text.
Unlike the Alexandrians, it was not the case that the inherent
literary needs of a work were invoked to explain the significance of
some puzzling or disconcerting feature.

The exegetical doctrines of the Stoics had interesting parallels
in their linguistic theory. For the Stoics, language, as it existed in
their own day, had by the passage of time been deeply corrupted
from its original, authentic form. This belief manifested itself in
two distinct ways. First, the Stoics, led by this conviction, devoted
a great deal of attention to what they called *etymologia*, that is
the search for *etyma*, or the primal, undistorted forms of words.
Second, the Stoics were committed Anomalists in the notorious

Analogist-Anomalist controversy of the Hellenistic period. This
meant that, in contrast to the Alexandrians (here, again, a consistent difference) they saw the language of their own day as
ultimately unsusceptible to rational, systematic analysis and
classification. Language was, *per se*, an anomalous phenomenon,
and could not be accounted for reasonably by systematic resort to
the principle of analogy, the explanatory tool employed by the
Alexandrians. The consequence was that language, like literature,
had little rational meaning in itself. In order for them to be understood, it was necessary for the philosopher to recover the uncor-
rupted, primal forms of both, in the case of early poetry those
truths which had been clad, for reasons suggested above, in the
garb of poetic language and deed. To be sure, the analogy between
poetry and language is not precise in that the source of "distortion"
is different in either case. In the former it is an intentional act of
"mystification" on the part of the poets, in the latter it is, apparently, the simple consequence of time. The resulting effect on
interpretative procedures was, however, very much the same.
As is the case with Aristarchus, the works of Crates and other
Stoic exegetes have come down in only fragmentary of derivative
form. The Homeric scholia contain much Stoic material, and both
in Cornutus' allegorical exposition, *Summary of Greek Theology*,
and in pseudo-Heraclitus' *Homeric Allegories* or *Problems* (the
former certainly, the latter probably, written in the first century
A.D.) there is much deriving from the early Stoics. Indeed, in
Heraclitus' work Crates' interpretations are referred to explicitly.

Further contributions to the allegorical tradition came from
the Jewish and Christian commentators on the Bible. The sources
are, of course, much more abundant here than with the Stoics and
include, in the case of the Jews, not only Rabbinic literature, in
particular the Biblical *midrashim*, but also the works of fully
Hellenized writers like Philo of Alexandria, and, in the case of the
Christians, a veritable ocean of commentary and interpretation.
In the face of such abundance, any effort at simplification becomes distinctly hazardous, but scholarly investigation suggests
that the Jews, and following their lead, the Christians, made certain
specific innovations in the theory of the allegorical reading of
texts. Prompted by obvious doctrinal motives, Jewish and
Christian interpreters insisted, first of all, with an all but unanimous
voice, that under no circumstances must the literal, i.e. historical,

sense of the biblical text be surrendered. Philo, for all his clear indebtedness to the Stoics allegorists for methods of interpretation, separated himself in this matter from his pagan masters in a quite unmistakable way, since, at least so far as the extant evidence goes, an insistence on the historicity of the Homeric or other poems was not a significant element in pagan allegorization. A second feature which appears to mark a departure from earlier practice, and here the evidence is less firm on the pagan side, is the development of what is generally called *typological* interpretation, i.e., the belief that some figure or event of the historical past should be understood as a *type*, a general form as it were, which prefigures an event yet to come or a person yet to be born. Thus for the Christians, Adam was the type of Christ, and for the Jewish Fathers, the episode of Jacob's Ladder prefigured the construction of the Temple in Jerusalem and the creation of the Temple priesthood.

The last great movement of antiquity in which allegorism played a vital part was Neoplatonism itself, and as Neoplatonic allegorism is one subject of the present study, little need be said now except that, apart from certain specific theoretical discoveries—and there do appear to have been such—the truly significant contribution of Neoplatonism was the systematic philosophical analysis to which they subjected the very process itself of allegorism. For at no earlier time, at least so far as the evidence allows us to form an opinion, did the practitioners of allegory produce so varied and satisfactory a body of theoretical insights in support of their own activities. Earlier writers were not without "theory," but with the Neoplatonists it is clear that allegorical interpretation had attained a new level of theoretical refinement and rigor.[21]

---

[21] On the subject of ancient allegory the following articles and books are useful guides. Those marked with asterisks are especially rich in bibliography: A. Altman, 'Bible: Allegorical Interpretations,' *Encyclopedia Judaica*, vol. 3 (Jerusalem, 1971), 895-899; M. von Albrecht, 'Allegorie,' *Lexikon der alten Welt* (Zurich, 1965), 121-124*; F. Buffière, *Les mythes d'Homère et la pensée grecque* (Paris, 1965)*; H. Dörrie, 'Zur Methodik antiker Exegese,' *Zeitschrift für die neutestamentliche Wissenschaft* 65 (1974), 121-138; A. Fletcher, 'Allegory,' *Dictionary of the History of Ideas*, vol. 1 (New York, 1968), 41-48*; J. Kaufmann, 'Allegorie,' *Encyclopedia Judaica*, vol. 2 (Berlin, 1928), 335-338; J. Pépin, *Mythe et allégorie* (Paris, 1958)*; B. Smalley, *The Study of the Bible in the Middle Ages* (Oxford, 1952); E. Stein, 'Allegorische Auslegung,' *Encyclopedia Judaica*, vol. 2 (Berlin, 1928), 338-351; J. Waszink, 'Allegorese,' *Reallexikon für Antike und Christentum*,

To return, it needs to be pointed out last of all that although the tradition of allegorism was a strong influence, and although the allegorically minded Neoplatonists themselves, for reasons I have tried to suggest, were not likely to find the methods and assumptions of rhetorical criticism congenial, there are nonetheless a number of passages in the commentaries where stylistic analysis is found in a form not very different from what we see in the works of a critic like Dionysius of Halicarnassus of "Longinus." Given the universality of rhetorical education in the ancient world, anything else would, in fact, have been surprising.

In trying to present the contributions of the Neoplatonic commentators to the history of ancient literary thought I have found it convenient to arrange their views under three broad headings. The first subject we shall examine is that of *representation*, or *mimesis*. In this matter the Neoplatonists proposed solutions to stubborn critical problems which deserve considerably more scholarly attention than they have received. This is true in particular of Proclus' distinction between what he terms *symbolic* and *eiconic* mimesis, a distinction which anticipates in certain important ways that made between allegory and symbol by critics like Goethe and Coleridge.[22] The second subject to be considered is that of *unity*. Here, too, the commentators worked out valuable distinctions, above all that between what I call a unity of *parts* and a unity of *levels*. The last broad critical concept to be examined is that of *literary organicism*, that is, the assumption that a work of literature is in some fundamental way analogous to a living organism. The belief had, of course, been long established, but the Neoplatonist synthesis brought it into conjunction with other philosophical beliefs, above all that which assumed an analogy between the macrocosmic Demiurge and the microcosmic literary artisan. In so doing they gave voice to a literary idea which has shown an abiding power and fruitfulness.[23]

---

vol. 1 (Stuttgart, 1950), 283-293*'; J. Werner, 'Allegorische Dichtererklärung,' *Der kleine Pauly*, vol. 2 (Stuttgart, 1964), 274.

[22] See René Wellek's convenient discussion, 'Symbol and Symbolism in Literature,' *Dictionary of the History of Ideas*, vol. 4, ed. Ph. Wiener (New York, 1973), 337-345.

[23] There is a stimulating examination of the influence on aesthetic theory of the analogy between God the creator and the human artist (both literary and other) in Milton Nahm's *The Artist as Creator* (Baltimore, 1956), especially Book I, *The Great Analogy* (pp. 3-209).

Finally, a word about the form of each chapter. Although my study is not intended, in the first instance, to be an historical or evolutionary treatment of the critical ideas under examination— my aim, rather, is to present in a systematic form these ideas as they work in the commentaries—I have nonetheless begun each chapter with a sketch of the major critical ideas which figured significantly in the Neoplatonists' theories. (I have also, for reasons of contrast, outlined major alternative solutions to the critical difficulties in question.) This procedure has been followed simply from the belief that if the reader has some grasp of the traditional attitudes or premises with which Neoplatonists themselves were familiar and found most congenial, the effort of a sympathetic understanding of the Neoplatonists' own ideas will be made that much easier. The question of originality, in some ways a difficult and, perhaps, even irrelevant one, will therefore not play an important role. I believe, of course, that in their commentaries the Neoplatonists had something to say which was new and of value. The question, however, of whether some specific detail in the Neoplatonic synthesis was anticipated or can be paralleled elsewhere is not one to which my efforts have been primarily directed. In particular, for reasons I have already indicated in the Introduction, I have considered neither the question of parallel developments in Christian and Neoplatonic exegesis nor the unlikely possibility that certain interpretative procedures attested in the Neoplatonic commentaries may have found their source in early Christian allegorization.

CHAPTER TWO

MIMESIS: EICON AND SYMBOL

1. PLATO AND ARISTOTLE

As we saw in the first chapter, ancient speculation on mimesis concerned itself, in general, with two questions. What, first, was the nature or status of the *object* of representation? Was it tangible and visible? Or was it something perceived in the artist's mind? In this case, was it a creation of his own fantasy, or was it something accessible to all human minds, some preexisting intelligible entity or some formal structure, such as necessity or probability, which was thought to inhere in concrete reality? If the visible, phenomenal world was being rendered, what was its ontological status or ethical worth? Could such a model be really real? Were the objects selected by the artist for representation ethically acceptable?

The second question had to do with the nature and, in some cases, the very value of the *process of representation itself*. How, it was asked, is representation effected? When a concrete entity or scene is being portrayed, the matter is, or seems, straightforward enough. But how, in fact, does one "copy" or "represent" in a visible medium something, such as an idea or abstraction, which is not perceived by the physical eye? And as regards artistic representation, *per se*, is it arguable that the experience itself on the part of the audience contains features inherently either beneficial or harmful? [1]

Plato's views on these questions are well known. Nonetheless, in the matter of his mimetic theories it is perhaps necessary to distinguish between what may be called his "official" or, at least, most widely known doctrines, those of the *Republic*, and, on the other hand, a body of scattered remarks whose tendency run in some respects quite counter to those doctrines. In this latter

---

[1] The following are useful general introductions to the subject of mimesis in the ancient world: H. Koller, *Mimesis in der Antike* (Bern, 1954); D. W. Lucas in Appendix I to his edition of Aristotle's *Poetics* (Oxford, 1968), 258-272; Göran Sörbom, *Mimesis and Art* (Uppsala, 1966); W. J. Verdenius, *Mimesis* (Leiden, 1949).

category one must include the theory of art which is implicit in Plato's own practice as a writer.[2]

Now the analysis of artistic representation (*mimesis*) set forth in Books II-III and X of the *Republic* is, I think, straightforward enough if we keep in mind the fact that the discussions in Books II-III, on the one hand, and in Book X, on the other, arise from different perspectives. That of Books II-III derives almost exclusively from a concern with the effect of literature on the ethical opinions or attitudes of the audience. Put in terms of Plato's philosophical views, it is an analysis of literature which reflects his belief that literature is necessarily a medium of opinion, not truth. For literature is limited, by its very non-dialectical nature, to the conveying of opinion only. The various forms of literature seem to be for Plato simply special instances of those dialectically unsupported (though not always, in theory, unsupportable) kinds of statements, i.e. opinions, which all of us regularly make about a number of important matters. Opinions, however, can be true or false, or, in ethical terms, good or bad. The content of literature must therefore be supervised with an eye to the ethical values implicit in the narrative or dramatic action. And attention must also be paid to the form of literature, since this too has ethical consequences. In Plato's judgment, certain meters and musical modes and, what is more immediately pertinent to our subject, certain forms of representation (e.g. dramatic as opposed to narrative) are demonstrably less appropriate than others to the task of educating the guardians, whose training is the subject of Books II-V.

These same categories, form and content, recur in Book X, but now from a new perspective, that of the philosopher who has gained a knowledge of the world of Forms. To put this matter briefly, for the philosopher artistic representation, literary or otherwise, has ultimately no value. It is a copy of a copy, and is at one further remove from reality than the world of objects and

---

[2] For an account of Plato's mimetic theories, there may be added to the studies cited in note 1 the following article: Richard McKeon, 'Literary criticism and the concept of imitation in antiquity,' *Modern Philology* 34 (1936) 1-35; repr. in *Critics and Criticism*, ed. R. Crane (Chicago, 1952). For discussions of Plato as a writer the following are useful: L. Edelstein, 'The function of the myth in Plato's philosophy,' *Journal of the History of Ideas*, 10 (1949), 463-481; G. Morrow, *Plato's Cretan City* (Princeton, 1960); P. Friedländer, *Plato*, vol. 1, tr. H. Meyerhoff (New York, 1958), 108-210.

events it represents. And added to this is the fact that the very *experience* of poetic representation on the part of the listener fortifies those same psychic dispositions which already all too powerfully impede our perception of the world of Forms. As regards Plato's judgment, then, concerning the nature and worth of artistic representation, we may say that at best literature in the context of non-philosophical education or persuasion has some value if properly supervised by the philosopher. But for the philosopher himself literature is both potentially harmful to his development and ultimately irrelevant.

The attentive reader of Plato, however, and we can assume that the Neoplatonists were such, may discern the outlines of a somewhat different position, one which, in fact, embraces the possibility that a certain kind of artist will be able to create with his eyes directly on intelligible reality, rather than on the intervening screen of visible phenomena. What I am suggesting, that Plato in some manner espouses what should properly be called an allegorical theory of art, is, at first hearing, a somewhat surprising notion. For is it not true that Plato, in the *Republic*, explicitly rejects any recourse to allegorical interpretation as a means to justifying what he considers the moral enormities of traditional myth? As has been convincingly pointed out by Tate, however, Plato nowhere denies the *existence* of allegorical "undersenses"; he simply insists that it does no good, when we are talking about the education of children, to invoke such palliatives, since children are primarily affected by the concrete events of narrative (*logos*) and by the norms of conduct implicit in them (*typos*) (II.376E-378E). On the strength of this passage alone, however, the question of Plato's own belief concerning the existence of allegory as a representational mode is unclear. But there are other indications to help us.[3]

The first of these is Plato's own practice. Now, it is probably correct that we should not view myths such as those at the end of the *Phaedo* or the 'likely tale' of Timaeus the Locrian concerning the origin and structure of the cosmos as in any strict way allegorical, at least in the sense defined above. Their nature and functions appear rather different. The former seems to aim at soothing

---

[3] For the question of Plato's attitude toward allegory, see J. Tate's excellent discussion, 'Plato and allegorical interpretation,' *Classical Quarterly* 23 (1929), 142-154 and 24 (1930), 1-10.

those portions—irrational and childlike—of the soul which are by
their very nature impervious to rational argument. To do this,
Socrates takes the 'noble risk' (*Phaedo* 114D) of composing an
account of the afterworld which, although not meant to be taken
as literally true in its specific details, yet in no way runs counter to
what dialectic has demonstrated about the nature and destiny of
the soul. In the same way, because of a firm belief of Plato that no
science of the physical world is possible, i.e. of the world of phenomenal change, the best that the philosopher can do is to construct
a "probable account," a "likely story." This is based on truth,
but is in no sense a direct rendering of it; rather, truth provides
the general outlines from which the philosopher-poet takes imaginative wing. Such myths as those of the *Phaedo* and the *Timaeus* are
thus, like literature in general for Plato, a kind of second best
pursuit—"charms" and "diversions," necessary only because of
human weakness. In the philosopher's hands, or under the philosopher's supervision, they will do no harm, and may even help in
certain circumscribed ways, so long as it is understood that they
can never take the place of the philosopher's proper pursuit, that
is, dialectic.[4]

Myths like that of the charioteer in the *Phaedrus*, however, or
those of the Cave or the Three Metals in the *Republic*, are of a
rather different nature. They share the characteristic with the
preceding species of myth that they presuppose certain human
limitations, and are thus of restricted value, but they differ in that
unlike the class of myths we have been discussing, for whose
specific elements no precise models, intelligible or otherwise, are
assumed necessarily to preexist, myths like those of the charioteer
are quite clearly attempts at rendering, in visible form, intelligible
entities whose reality the philosopher has perceived with his
mind's eye. They are thus quite undeniably allegorical in character,
since they do have, to use Plato's word, a clear "undersense."
The charioteer and the two horses, for example, are simply an
eikon which "images" the structure of the human soul. The charioteer is an image of the rational part of the soul, the white horse of
the "spirited," and so on.[5]

---

[4] See especially Edelstein, *op. cit.* (*supra*, n. 2).

[5] As Plato says (*Phaedrus* 246A), we cannot, without a "divine and
extended account," tell what the real nature of the soul *is*, but we can say
what it is *like* (*eoiken, eoiketo*).

Now, the existence of such clearly allegorical myths should not surprise us, for there are sufficient indications that Plato did in fact propose such forms of myth. First, and most important of all, is the evidence of the *Gorgias* and the *Phaedrus* as regards rhetoric, and of the *Republic* as regards poetry. In these three dialogues, a higher, i.e. philosophical, species of either literary form is outlined or, at least, hinted at. Under "ideal" conditions both will be practiced either by the philosopher himself (Socrates in the eschatological myths of the *Gorgias* and *Phaedrus*) or by artists directly under the supervision of the philosopher (*Republic*). In either case, rhetorician and poet, the latter of whom may, it is true, occasionally by inspiration 'lay hold of the truth' (*Laws* III. 682A), i.e. true opinion, will not be allowed to pursue their own crafts independently of the philosopher, since poet and rhetorician without such direction are, in Plato's eyes, no more than purveyors of false opinion or contemptible "copiers" of the murky world of visible phenomena. As regards Plato's views, it is a mistake to believe that the rhetorician should be sharply distinguished from the poet. We should recall, for one thing, that Socrates' great speeches in the "rhetorical" dialogues, *Gorgias* and *Phaedrus*, are mythic narratives, indeed prose poems about the fate of the soul when it is free of the body. And conversely, much poetry in Greek, like other, literature is cast in the form of people not only acting, but *speaking*—whether to "us" or to other characters—, and the Greek critical tendency, evident also in Plato, was to see no essential difference between these poetic forms of speech-making and the more obviously "rhetorical" kinds of speech. Moreover, in the schema of reformed arts outlined in the *Republic* not only edifying exampla or protreptic myth would figure; strictly allegorical myths, such as those of the charioteer or the three metals, would also, surely, play some role.[6]

Another strand of Plato's thought which helped to create the presumption of a Plato who looked favorably on allegory was his attitude toward divine inspiration in the poets. For if a poet *is* divinely inspired, how can the product of this inspiration be assigned a less than an exalted status? This is not the place to

---

[6] The fact that a myth such as that of the three metals might not necessarily be "read" allegorically by those for whom it was intended does not mean that it was not conceived in such a mode by the philosopher-rulers of the state.

argue the matter out, but is does seem that although Plato is
often ironical at the poet's expense, it is almost certainly not
because he does not believe that they are sometimes divinely
inspired. He clearly does, it seems to me. What he is ironical
about is the poet's claim to *knowledge*. Plato may allow that poets,
on occasion, do hit upon the truth. But by what criterion are we to
tell when this is the case? And even if we could infallibly do so,
we are still left with the difficulty that what the poets communicate
to us would be simply *true opinion*. This is, of course, superior to
false opinion, but the philosopher cannot really afford the status
of knowledge to anything except what is arrived at by dialectic,
since knowledge is true opinion supported by logos. Because of
this the poet is really of no ultimate use to the philosopher. This
does not mean, however, that he is not at times genuinely inspired.
Plato was quite unironical on this point. As often happens, however,
a carefully qualified position was often extended, even misinterpreted, in a way that would no doubt have disturbed its formulator.
Nonetheless, part of the responsibility is Plato's, since it is in some
respects difficult, even if not logically so, to reconcile an ironical
attitude toward the god-filled poets with the deeply felt convictions
about the divine which Plato everywhere manifests. Plato's
enthusiastic description of divine possession therefore, once stripped
of his qualifications, proved an immensely powerful support for a
continued reverence for the wisdom of the poets. Thus, this strand
too of Plato's thought, although in a different way, contributed
importantly to a theory of allegory.[7]

Most important of all, perhaps, is the fact that Plato's philosophy,
as has been well pointed out by Pépin, is allegorical in its very
basic assumptions. In Plato's metaphysics, the visible world is
conceived of as a surface image "reflecting" or "participating in"
or "caused by" a transcendental order of being. In this view,
whatever the precise ontological model, the world is a veil which we
are invited to lift aside, a riddle whose answer we are asked to
conjecture. This world has no meaning or existence in itself;
it is there to be fathomed, and then left behind. Thus, and in

---

[7] The following is a useful discussion of Plato's views on poetical inspiration: E. N. Tigerstedt, *Plato's Idea of Poetical Inspiration* (= Commentationes Humanarum Litt., Societas Scientiarum Fennica, vol. 44) (Helsinki,
1969). As is clear from European criticism from the Renaissance onwards,
the same ambiguities have also been exploited by modern critics.

a quite different sense than is usually maintained, Plato really should be thought of as the father of allegory, not because allegory, as has sometimes been mistakenly argued, began as a reaction to his strictures against the poets, but because the view of the world he left to posterity was deeply congenial to the allegorical mentality. This is borne out by the fact that it was precisely those schools of thought most influenced by or sympathetic to aspects of Platonic thought which pursued allegorical interpretation in a large-scale and consistent fashion, i.e. the Stoics (especially as regards theories of poetry and language), the Neoplatonists and the Platonizing Christians, such as the Alexandrian and Cappadocian Fathers.

In Aristotle, too, we find answers to the problems we formulated at the beginning of this chapter. But they derive from a very different conception of reality and generate, therefore, a different aesthetic, one quite uncongenial to an allegorical view of literature. Allegory presupposes, on the conceptual and analytical levels at least, a clear separation between copy and model. In Aristotle's view, however, and here he differed from Plato, form could not be divorced from matter; therefore, such a separation in literature was also philosophically unlikely. In Aristotle's philosophical system, there were, to be sure, formal categories, such as probability and necessity, but these had simply a potential existence, and it was only when embodied in concrete narrative or dramatic details at the hands of a gifted poet that they were actualized. Now both Plato and Aristotle viewed drama and epic, understandably enough, as representations of men in action, but there was an all-important difference between the two in the way this fact was understood. For Plato, as we saw, there exist *a priori* ethical categories, forms, let us say, of justice or of courage. These were, in theory at least, rationally definable by the philosopher and existed apart from our world in the fullest degree of being. And it is only by a knowledge of these forms, either directly or through the mediation of the pilosopher, that true narratives can be created, as it is only by reference to forms that we are enabled to judge whether a work of literature is a true or false representation or, in other Platonic terms, whether it conveys true or false opinions. In Aristotle's philosophy, however, although the concepts of probability and necessity *can* obviously be thought of as enjoying a separate, formal existence, they were of interest to the theoretician of literature only when actualized in specific literary structures. They do not reside, as do the forms for Plato, in a higher realm of being, self-sufficient objects of contemplation. For Plato, the contemplation of forms *in themselves* is the highest goal of the philosopher's life. As a consequence, literature must be viewed as, at best, only a dim and unsatisfactory rendering of this world. Literature, in the end, is expendable. But this is untrue of Aristotle in a very specific way, since in the case of a tragedy like the *Oedipus Rex* there are no prior forms or models of which the actions or thoughts in Sophocles' play are copies. What did preexist, to be embodied by Sophocles to an overwhelmingly successful degree, were universal structures of probable or necessary actions. They were only potential categories, however, and needed a Sophocles to give them actual, embodied form. The play is consequently *more real* than anything which preceded it—a view which is clearly the direct antithesis to that of Plato. Obviously, such a conception of literature is radically uncongenial to allegorical thinking, and, in fact, Aristotle cannot be demonstrated to gave played much of a role in the later allegorical tradition.[8]

2. NEOPLATONIC CONTRIBUTIONS

Despite the formidable impulse which Plato's analysis of literature gave to speculation about the nature of allegorical representation, a number of problems remained. For example, when interpreting "Platonic" allegories (such as *Cebes' Tablet* of the Hellenistic era), what is being represented by the details of the narrative is generally clear, as is the mechanism by which the representation is effected. The former is the world of intelligible reality, of eternal and immutable ideas. The latter may be described as a kind of multiple, one-to-one correspondence between elements of the intelligible and sensible world. That is to say, each of the numerous elements of the narrative corresponds, singly, to some single counterpart in the realm of ideas and abstractions. It is the sort of allegory we saw in the *Phaedrus* where the white horse represents the spirited part of the soul, the black horse the appeti-

---

[8] For a discussion of these points, see V. Galli, 'La mimesi artistica secondo Aristotele,' *Studi Italiani di Filologia Classica*, N.S., 4 (1926), 281-390, esp. 310, 373-376. For a glimpse of Aristotle as a user of allegorical methods, see Eustathius (ed. Stallbaum) on *Odyssey* 12.129, where Aristotle's interpretation of the Cattle of the Sun is given.

tive, the charioteer the rational. For the ancients, however, there were other, less transparent kinds of myths, such as those that are found in Homer and the Bible. Here the question of the relationship between what we see and what we conjecture to be the model, or models, is a rather puzzling one. It is clearly not a case of what I have just termed a multiple, one-to-one correspondence. For how could the various elements of the passionate and turbulent world of Homeric myth simply "stand for" or "represent" an unchanging set of intelligible realities which the interpreters believed they did? There is a further, related difficulty, and that is that in the case of this species of myth there are often several, apparently equally justifiable interpretations. Now the allegorical view of literature, as we saw in the introduction, goes closely in hand with a belief in intention. But how do we *know* that a myth is meant to be read allegorically? How, in other words, do we know that some *intention* lies behind the paradoxical and turbulent surface of a mythic fiction? These are some of the questions for which the Neoplatonists, and Proclus in particular, attempted to find solutions.

Let us turn first to Proclus' commentary on the *Timaeus*.[9] This is the one work of his we can date with exactness; we are told by Marinus, his pupil, that it was composed in Proclus' twenty-seventh year, i.e. almost certainly in 439 A.D. And if the conjecture of Saffrèy and Westerink concerning the date of Syrianus' death is correct, it will have been written by Proclus shortly after the death of his master, to whose interpretations Proclus' acknowledgments in this commentary are open and frequent. The part of the commentary which will concern us first is that in which Proclus is interpreting two portions of the opening scene of the *Timaeus*, i.e., Socrates' "recapitulation" of the argument of the *Republic*

---

[9] Apart from the splendid translation with notes of the *Timaeus* commentary by Festugière, which is cited in the Bibliography, one should also consult his earlier article, 'Modes des compositions des Commentaires de Proclus,' in *Museum Helveticum*, 20 (1963), 77-100. Also still useful, if only because it contains summaries of the commentaries of Proclus, is T. Whittaker, *The Neo-Platonists* [2] (Cambridge, 1928) 229-314. I was not able to find the following article: Tanaka, 'What we owe to ancient and what to modern commentators, with special reference to Proclus,' *Journal of Classical Studies*, Kyoto University (1953). For the likely date of the composition of the *Timaeus* commentary, see H. D. Saffrey and L. G. Westerink in the introduction (xvi-xvii) to the first volume of their edition of Proclus' *Platonic Theology* (Paris, 1968). The "recapitulation" of the *Republic* at the beginning has been much discussed; see F. M. Cornford, *Plato's Cosmology* (London, 1937), 3-5.

and then, the story of Atlantis narrated by Critias (17B-25D). The character of either narration is distinct: the one is a sober sketch, brief and schematic, of the structure of the reformed Greek *polis* which Socrates had elaborated in a previous discussion; Critias's tale, on the other hand, is an extravagant and dramatic legend, set some nine thousand years before the speaker's own time. According to Proclus, the chief question which had vexed previous commentators was whether one was to take this initial section containing the two narratives "more ethically" (*ethikoteron*), i.e. as intended to predispose the reader's *character* to a more ready understanding of the main, physical portion of the dialogue to follow. Or was it rather, as some others, apparently "Pythagorean" in sympathy, had maintained, a preliminary "representation" (*mimesis*) of what was to follow, offered to the reader first (i.e. in Socrates' sketch) in the form of an "explicit rendering" (*delosis*) conveyed "through likenesses and images (*eikones*) of the matters under investigation," and, then, through a "secret hinting" (*endeixis aporrhetos*) of these same matters, communicated now by means of what Proclus calls *symbola*.

> "And so, the recapitulation of the *Republic* which appears before the section on physics addresses itself to a consideration of the structure of the universe by means of likenesses (*eikonikōs*); the story of the Atlantis does the same, but by means of symbols (*symbolikōs*). Indeed, it is by means of symbols that myths customarily hint at higher realities. Consequently, although physics is the subject of the whole dialogue, it is presented one way in one place, and another way in another."
> (I. 130.11-8)

The same distinction between *symbolon* and *eikon* recurs later.[10] The basis for the distinction, however, is not yet made entirely explicit by Proclus in the work under discussion. We shall have to wait for the *Republic* commentary for that.[11] But there are enough

---

[10] Book II.205.1-16, 355.19-20.

[11] Apart from the translation of the *Republic* commentary, with notes by Festugière, which is cited in the Bibliography, there are older works which are still valuable. On the relative chronology of the various essays which will make up the commentary, see, Gallavotti, 'Eterogeneità e cronologia dei commenti di Proclo alla *Repubblica*,' *Rivista di filologia* 57, n.s. 7 (1929), 208-219, esp. 210-213. Rather difficult to find, but nonetheless useful in their treatment of various points in the present chapter, are the following: Ansgar Friedl, *Die Homer-Interpretationen des Neuplatonikers Proklos* (Diss., Würzburg, 1936); Carlo Gallavotti, 'L'estetica greca nell' ultimo suo

hints so that with the proleptic aid of the *Republic* commentary we can elucidate some of the distinctive features of either mode of narration. If we take together the two passages we cited above (I. 30.11-18, II. 205.1-16), we may state the following. The *Republic* "resumé" portrays the structure of the universe through the medium of "likenesses" and "images." Socrates' sketch of the ideal state, in some way "fit" or "was congruent to (*ephermoze*) the structure of the universe" (205.10). It is a *delosis* as opposed to an *endeixis aporrhetos*; that is, it reveals directly rather than hinting at secretly. The latter is characteristic of the symbolic mode. Both the symbolic and eiconic modes serve the same end in this dialogue, that of portraying Platonic physics, but they do so in different ways (*diaphoroi tropoi tes paradoseos*, 30.17-18). For while the ideal state as outlined by Socrates bears a *likeness* to the organization of the cosmos, the legend of the struggle between the inhabitants of Atlantis and the primordial citizens of Athens seems on the face of it to show no such similarity.

It is important at this point to try to clear up the ambiguities in the terms "like" and "likeness." In English we mean something obviously different when we say, "This picture isn't *like* you" and when we say, "Mooring a ship is *like* parking a car." The first is a relationship of *replica* or *facsimile*; the second, an analogically grounded similarity. The Greek terms used by Proclus here (i.e. *homoia* and *eikon*) are marked by the same ambiguities. Thus, when Proclus says Socrates' recapitulation is a "likeness" (*eikon*) of the structure of the universe, he clearly does *not* mean that it is a portrait (*eikon* can mean that) of that structure, but, rather, that it is like, or analogous, to that structure and that it enjoys, as well, a relationship of likeness which is direct and obvious, as was the case in our example of parking and mooring or of Plato's myth of the charioteer in the *Phaedrus*. This representational relationship is essentially what Proclus means by eiconic mimesis and it is very close to the modern sense of the critical term allegory. As far as the symbolic mode of representation is concerned, it may be noted in a preliminary way that although the mechanism of likeness or correspondence, as we shall see, figures, and importantly so, there is no question of a one-to-one likeness between copy and model which is also direct and obvious. Indeed, it is a prime characteristic of the symbol that it seems quite "unlike" what it represents, so much so, in fact, that Proclus is compelled to speak of it as only "hinting secretly" at what it ultimately represents. Proclus is also saying, to state the matter from a different angle, that the fabulous and romantic nature of the struggle between Atlantis and Athens or, in the Homeric poems, the portrayals of divinities as driven turbulently by all-too-human emotions, proclaim, *by these very features*, that they are to be taken as symbols which demand our interpretation.

The symbol hints, but because it hints it also hides. And what is concealed is related to what is revealed by unseen correspondences:

> "Plato understood this (i.e. the invisible structure of the cosmos), and through the medium of symbols and riddles represents for us (i.e. in the Atlantis story) the character of the elements which are in the universe, and the manner in which, through the intellectual activity (*noera energeia*) of Athena, the weaker is subordinated to the stronger. It is with good reason, then, that Plato recalled the deeds of the Athenians, for he knew that the whole universe was pervaded by that kind of analogy (i.e. by a process corresponding in its own way to the elements of the Atlantis story)."
> (132.21-27)

As has already been suggested, the symbol was an important constituent in the literary theory of the Neoplatonists, especially that of Proclus. In an appendix to the present chapter (App. I), the history of the term is discussed in greater detail, but it does seem useful, for the present, to outline in a briefer way the chief features of that discussion in order to place the various matters which will soon arise into a more systematic framework.

The word *symbolon*, which was to become a favored term in Neoplatonic allegorical exegesis, originally denoted a "token of identification," a sign of some relationship, such as that of guest-friendship or, perhaps, some commercial agreement. Often, it was in the form of an incomplete half of some concrete object, such as a die, which was later to be joined (*symbolon* has the same root as the Greek verb, *symballein*, meaning 'join') to the other half as proof of identity or purpose. In time, the word, by metaphorical extension, was applied to any object, word, or event whose significance was not readily self-evident (and therefore somehow intriguing) and which also, for that reason, required for its interpretation some special prior knowledge on the part of the interpreter. For example, the beacon-light in the *Agamemnon* signalling to those who knew the return of the Greeks from Troy was called a *symbolon*, as were also various prophetic signs to which the Greeks and all ancient peoples were especially alive. To what may be called the suggestive incompleteness or hinting power and the necessity for prior knowledge for interpretation there should be added a third attribute of the symbol, and that is that its significance, and the possibility of its interpretation, frequently rest on the mechanism of correspondence. ^The symbol in its original concrete form, as we saw, reveals its meaning through the fact that one of its halves fits in with or corresponds to the other. So, too, in more developed symbolic interpretation, water, for example, because it is the most "formless" of all the elements of nature, is taken in Neoplatonic exegesis as a symbol of the phenomenal world, since the ever-changing aspect of large bodies of water, and its consequent remoteness from any kind of fixed form, *corresponds* in a clear way to the material world with its ultimate multiplicity and deprivation of being (i.e. form).

Although the word *symbolon* came to be used extensively by the allegorical interpreters, to whom we shall devote the major part of our attention, it also had a small place in the rhetorical tradition. In general, the conceptions of literature shared by the rhetorical critics differed, as we saw in Chapter One, in a number of fundamental respects from those of allegorically minded commentators. Nonetheless, there were several notions elaborated by the rhetorical critics which found a place among the allegorists; among them was that group of figures and tropes which shared the common characteristic that the writers who employed them were thought of as saying one thing, but meaning something else. It is precisely in this sense, that denoted by the much more common term *allegoria*, that the critic Demetrius (*On Style* 243) uses the word *symbolon*.

It is chiefly in the allegorical tradition, however, that *symbolon* achieves the status of a major critical concept. Very briefly, the contexts in which the word was used and the interpretational problems which this use was designed to resolve, were something like the following. If a passage in a mythic narrative, Homer or the Bible, let us say, contained some disquieting or paradoxical feature and was thought because of that fact to be hinting to the reader that it was the author's intention that the narrative be taken at more than face-value, it was the habit of the allegorical critics to characterize such a passage as "symbolic" and to give the name "symbol" to those kinds of features which I have just described. The attribution of symbolic status to elements of a text, therefore, rested on, among other things, the assumption that literary texts were to be read as an *intentional* form of communication and that the reader was chiefly alerted to that intention by symbols consciously employed by the author. Although the recognition of the presence, *per se*, of a given symbol seemed to involve few difficulties, the question of how to interpret the intention lying behind the symbol was another matter. Briefly, the difficulty lay in the fact that commentators regularly assumed that a symbol was capable of several simultaneously true but seemingly divergent interpretations. Of course, many critics since have assumed the same, but the question was nonetheless handled in a rather careless fashion before the Neoplatonists of the fourth century A.D. directed their attention to the matter. Finally, the key mechanism which the allegorical critics employed in the interpretation of a text which had declared itself to be symbolic was that of analogy or correspondence. Again and again, it is by the ladder of analogy that a commentator will ascend from the surface of the text to its hidden meaning.

In Proclus' commentary on the *Republic*, the elements we have been considering, both the earlier allegorical tradition and Proclus' own discussion of the *Timaeus*, are brought together with a suggestiveness and systematic rigor which entitle Proclus, as well as his teacher, Syrianus, to a position of importance in the history of ancient literary theory, above all in the matter of the distinction between eiconic and symbolic mimesis. For in this Proclus seemingly anticipated the important distinction between allegory and symbol, whose formulation is customarily assigned by historians of literary theory to critics of the late eighteenth and early nineteenth century. The commentary on the *Republic* is a work which differs in character from the other extant commentaries of Proclus. In these the traditional format of lemma and appended commentary is followed; the present work is a collection of monographs, each devoted to a separate portion of the *Republic* (The lemma form, however, is sometimes also followed in individual monographs). The essays which concern us are found on pp. 42-205 of the first volume of Kroll's edition. The first essay, *Plato's Doctrines on Poetry and its Various Kinds, and The Best Harmony and Rhythm* (pp. 42-69),

will not enter into our discussion for the most part. It is immeasurab-
ly less important, and was probably written rather earlier than the
second essay. This, *On What Plato Says in the Republic against
Homer and Poetry*, made up of two books, constitutes the most
serious attempt in antiquity, after Aristotle, to resolve the questions raised by Plato in the *Republic*. The method differs, of
course, *toto caelo* from that of Aristotle; his approach to the
problems raised by Plato was that of an independent thinker,
indebted to Plato for having isolated difficulties, but at the
same time convinced that the criticisms levelled by Plato
against poetry were the result of serious misunderstandings. A
critical position of this kind was really not conceivable for Proclus.
For the Neoplatonists Plato was, in a very real sense, a god and far
above criticism. But Homer was another god, and it was precisely
this fact which engendered their dilemma. If we take Plato's
criticism of Homer, and of poetry in general, at face value, what
are we then to do with the Homeric and Hesiodic poems, which
almost the whole of the ancient tradition concurred in viewing as
divinely inspired? [12] It was not open to Proclus to argue that
Plato was in error. He had to adopt another line. Plato was quite
serious, Proclus argues, in what he says about poetry in the *Republic*. But what he says is to be taken as applying only to *one* kind of
poetry. Plato is, in this sense, "ironic." As Socrates says in Book X,
poetry is to be rejected "to the extent that it is mimetic," i.e.
simply a photograph-like rendering of the external world. No
matter that, as some modern interpreters would argue, Plato's
category was coextensive with the whole of existing Greek poetry.[13]
Proclus uses Plato's ambiguously worded qualification as a key
to open up the back door and readmit Homer into the company of
philosophers. Proclus agrees that poetry, to the extent that it
is mimetic, is inappropriate to philosophical education. But

---

[12] For an appreciation of this dilemma, see Gallavotti, 'L'estetica greca,'
op. cit. (*supra*, n. 11), 42. The reader will find good treatments of ancient
attitudes toward Homer and Hesiod in the following works: F. Buffière,
Les mythes d'Homère et la pensée grecque (Paris, 1956); J. Pépin, *Mythe et
allégorie* (Paris, 1958). Neoplatonist philosophers such as Porphyry and
Proclus were also not inconsiderable Homeric and Hesiodic scholars; an
interested reader will find the following useful: R. Beutler, 'Proklos,' *RE*
23 (1957), 206-207; J. Pépin, 'Porphyre, exégète d'Homère,' *Entretiens sur
l'antiquité classique*, XII. *Porphyre* (Geneva, 1965), 195-228.

[13] For this view, see above all Eric Havelock, *Preface to Plato* (Cambridge,
U.S.A., 1963).

Homer's poetry, although, at times, undeniably mimetic, is also, Proclus argues, symbolic, and of a quite different order. It should therefore be understood as, to that extent, *not* falling under Plato's general proscription. Now, it is also true, in Proclus' view, that at certain times even symbolic poetry should be banned, but only, first of all, from the reach of those who because of limited faculties or training are incapable of seeing it as anything but mimetic, and who fail, therefore, to grasp its symbolic qualities. And, secondly, it should be kept from the young of the ideal state. For such as these it is admittedly inappropriate. These qualifications aside, however, it is the highest form of poetry.

In the following discussion of mimesis I do not intend to examine all aspects of Proclus' treatment of the matter. His essay is, in any case, at last available in Festugière's accurate translation. What will be examined is the cardinally important second chapter of the first book, *The Reasons for the Objections Which Have Been Made to the Manner in Which the Theologians (i.e. Homer et al.) Fashioned Their Myths and Answers to the Criticisms Made Against Them* (pp. 71-86).

The structure of this chapter, despite some obscurities, is sufficiently clear. After brief introductory remarks (71.21-72.9), Proclus restates two lines of criticism of the Homeric poems and of mythic literature in general. The first (72.9-74.4), essentially a recasting of Socrates' critique of Books II-III of the *Republic*, addresses itself to the inappropriateness of the Homeric stories to the divine nature and their consequent incapacity to "image" its "ineffable superiority":

> "For these symbols [14] (i.e. the words and actions of Homeric myth) will clearly not *resemble* the divine substances. The myths, therefore, if they are not to fall short completely of the truth which is in the divine beings, must somehow be made in the *likeness* of those realities the understanding of which they attempt to cover with the veil of visible reality."
> (73.11-16)

Proclus then puts into Socrates' mouth some recommendations concerning more acceptable alternatives. Myths about the gods, he says, should be like Plato's myths. These,

---

[14] See Festugière *ad loc.* for a discussion of the use of the word 'symbol' for the *actions* of Homeric myth.

"instruct us through the medium of *images* (*eikones*) on divine
matters in the way of the mysteries, and no shamefulness or suggestion of disorder or turbulent and material semblances (*phantasmata*) find their way into his myths. Rather, his thoughts are hidden,
undefiled; and placed before them, like visible statues made in the
likeness of things within them, are *likenesses* of his secret teaching."
(73.17-22) [15]

There are two points to be made. First, we should understand
the term "likeness" in these two passages in the sense we explicated
earlier in reference to Socrates' "recapitulation" of the *Republic*
at the beginning of the *Timaeus*. Proclus' comparison with statues
makes this clear, for by his time no one, at least no educated
person, supposed that statues of marble or bronze were "likenesses"
of gods in the sense that a portrait bust is a likeness of the man
who sat for it. Nonetheless, it was believed that qualities like
grandeur, omniscience, benevolence suggested by visible statues
were clearly *like* the attributes of that divine being who was the
"model" of the statue. Secondly, it is not clear which Platonic
myths Proclus has specifically in mind, but his reference to the
gods does make one think of, among others, the celestial myth
narrated by Socrates in his second speech in the *Phaedrus*. What is
noteworthy in that myth, too, is the unmistakable and immediate
likeness, or a appropriateness, of the various narrative elements to
the gods who are being portrayed. If I understand Proclus correctly, he is saying that Plato, as a creator of myths, is a writer
who works in the eiconic mode.[16] Indeed this is almost certainly
suggested by the opening lines of the second passage ("through
images") as well as by the unmistakable contrast with the supposed
characteristics of symbolic mimesis (misapprehended by our
imaginary critic) which are alluded to in the first passage. The
second class of criticism stems from unnamed contemporaries

---

[15] The categories *eikones* and *phantasmata* derive, of course, from a
passage in Plato's *Sophist* (235D-236C). For an account of the concepts of
eikon in early Christian thought, see: H. Merki, 'Ebenbildlichkeit,' *Reallexikon für antike und Christentum*, 4 (1959), 464-478. On this same matter
there is an interesting essay by G. Ladner, 'The concept of the image in the
Greek Fathers,' *Dumbarton Oaks Papers*, 7 (1953), 1-34.

[16] A seemingly inconsistent position, according to which Plato's myths
as examples of *symbolic* expression, is developed by Proclus in the opening
portion of his *Platonic Theology* (ed. Saffrey and Westerink): ch. 4, 18.25 ff;
p. 19, note 1; ch. 4, 21.1 ff.

(74.4-9), who assert that the traditional myths have contributed to public immorality.

Proclus takes up first this latter, and more easily disposed of, objection (74.9-76.17). The criticism, Proclus says, derives from two failures of understanding. First, such critics do not perceive the difference between that kind of myth which is purely fanciful invention (*plasma*) and that which is the bearer of a profound sense. They make the mistake of imputing to all species of myth the faults which characterize only its more trivial variety. The mysteries, too, Proclus asserts, and even drinking, both of which can serve noble purposes,[17] are likewise sometimes misused by those who do not understand their higher functions and are thus brought into disrepute.

Proclus' answer (76.17-86.23) to the second, i.e. Socrates', objections, are however of a different order and need to be examined in far greater detail. The foundation of Proclus' solution of the difficulties raised by Socrates is his theory of the two classes of myth, the *paideutic* and the *entheastic*, categories which correspond respectively to what have been called up to now the eiconic and symbolic.[18] The former, the "educative," is fashioned with the hearer's character or disposition (*hexis*) primarily in view. The purpose of the latter is to fashion representations of the whole of reality from its lowest material manifestations to highest unity. It is therefore necessary to recognize that the "lives" (76.28), i.e. states of soul, of those who are fit to experience either kind of myth are quite distinct. Paideutic myth is for those whose souls are still in the process of being formed. Entheastic myths, on the other hand, are appropriate to those 'lives' which are "able to be aroused to Intellect, to all the classes of gods, to the processions which unfold through all Being and to the chains and their extremities which eagerly extend themselves to the lowest order of being" (77.1-4).

We may begin our discussion of this mode of poetry by citing a passage at the end of the essay, in which Proclus draws together, in a striking way, the various strands in his discussion of entheastic or symbolic myth.

---

17 This is a reference, of course, to Laws I.646A ff.

18 By *paideutikos*, Proclus means 'educational,' by *entheastikos*, 'inspired.' The word 'entheastical' is attested in English (see *OED, s.v.*), but 'entheastic' is more in accord with modern usage.

"Since, therefore, such myths (i.e. as those of Homer) arouse
those naturally endowed to a longing for the knowledge hidden
within them, and by their grotesque surface (*ten phainomenen
teratologian*) provoke a search for the truth which has been set in its
shrine, while at the same time preventing profane individuals
from laying hands on what is forbidden for them to touch, *are
they not, in an outstanding way, appropriate to the very gods whose
substance they communicate to us*? For many are the races of beings
which have been placed before the gods (i.e. between them and men).
Some (i.e. the lowest) belong to the demonic orders, others to the
angelic. They (i.e., the demons) enthrall all who have been aroused
to perceive them and who have made themselves ready to perceive
the light, and raise them on high towards union with the gods.
*And one might best perceive the kinship of these myths with the race of
demons in the activity of the latter in making revelations to men
through the medium of symbols*, as happens when some of us during
waking hours encounter demons or when, in sleep, we have profited
from some inspiration from them by which there were revealed to
us many things in the past and in the future. *Now in all such fictions
found in the makers of myths, it is generally the case that one thing
is hinted at by another. In all that the poets convey to us by these means,
it is not a relationship of model to copy, but of symbol to something
else which has an affinity to it by virtue of analogy.* If therefore the
mode of mythic poetry is, in this way, demonic, must we not say
that it is far superior to all the various, other kinds of myth, both
that which looks toward nature and interprets physical forces, and
that which has undertaken to educate the character of our soul."
(85.26-86.23) [19]

The most important matter to note for the present is Proclus'
assertion that in symbolic poetry there is no question of a "relationship of model to copy," a characteristic, apparently, of eiconic
representation and paideutic myth. Rather, there is a mysterious
and much more complex relationship between the symbols of
mythic narrative, on the face of it often bizarre and monstrous,
and that divine world these symbols were thought to evoke. It is a
mysterious relationship because of the seeming unlikeness of the
symbol to that at the existence of which it secretly hints. Another
passage is illuminating:

"Symbols are not representations of those things of which they
are symbols. For that which is the contrary of something else cannot
be a representation of that thing, such as the ugly of the beautiful
or that which is contrary to nature of that which is natural. For

---

[19] For accounts of physical and moralizing allegories, see Buffière, *op. cit.*
(*supra*, n. 12), 79-227, 249-391 and Pépin, *ibid.*, 95-111, 125-131.

symbolic wisdom hints at the nature of reality through the medium of elements totally contrary in their nature."
(198.15-19)

It is also a *complex* relationship because, unlike paideutic myth, in which there exists only a one-to-one correspondence of directly and clearly similar copy and model, symbolic mimesis—without doubt, it was claimed by Proclus, the superior and more philosophical form of representation—possessed the capacity to suggest to the reader the whole structure of reality in all the complexity which the Neoplatonists believed it to possess. For the symbol was precisely that element which had the power to lead the reader out of the text on its lowest, "demonic" level and carry him all the way up to primal unity, traversing by analogically connected links, in the course of this movement, the whole intervening range of Being.[20]

There exists, as Proclus says, a relationship of "symbol to something else which has an affinity to it by virtue of analogy" (86.18). Now, the concept of analogy is of the greatest importance for understanding Proclus' theory of symbolic or entheastic myth. In Proclus' scheme of reality, the universe, both in its intelligible and visible forms, is conceived of as a vast array of "chains" or "series" radiating from a central, unified core. These chains, each of which bears the mark of some specific quality, proceed in a way analogous to the spreading of the sun's rays; there is never a gap in their radiation, but there is a diminishment of force, or "reality," the further any given point in the chain is removed from its source, i.e. the more unity "becomes" multiplicity. There is another way, however, according to Proclus, in which the same phenomenon can be viewed, and in this the analogy of the sun's rays no longer holds. For reality can be thought of as a reciprocal process: not only does the central, unified core of being unfold into multiplicity, but this multiplicity is, in turn, constantly "reverting" to its source. Indeed, from a third point of view, it is clear that the core of reality never either unfolds, or has what has

---

[20] There are good discussions of the survival of symbolic thought, often more or less directly derivative from Proclus, in the following studies: D. C. Allen, *Mysteriously Meant* (Baltimore, 1970); E. Gombrich, *Symbolic Images: Studies in the Art of the Renaissance* (London, 1972); R. Roques, 'Dionysius Areopagita,' *Reallexikon für Antike und Christentum* 3 (1957), 1075-1121, esp. 1105-1108, 'Dialektik der Symbole'; E. Wind, *Pagan Mysteries in the Renaissance* [2] (London, 1967), esp. 2-25.

unfolded return to it; it "remains" where it is. It seems quite
clear that these three processes were not thought of as possessing
distinct realities; rather they were seen as three aspects of the
same reality, all of them simultaneously true. Another difference
from the analogy of the radiating sun is that although the sun's
rays proceed in a uniform, unimpeded way, the chains of Proclan
reality are built out of a number of distinct vertical orders, sort
of way-stations, each lower one of diminishing reality. (Perhaps we
may see in this the conceptual analogue of the sun's diminishing
force.) Each of these orders, moreover, is triadically structured,
apparently in an attempt to combine the notion of transcendence of
each order as regards the one immediately below it with the further
notion that its reality also persisted at a lower level. For the
members of the triad, in one of the more common forms in which it is
found, were clearly devised with this end in view. The highest
member of the triad is that which is not "partaken of" (*to
amethekton*), i.e. it remains untouched, although it is the cause of
what follows it, both immediately and all the way down its particular "chain." The middle member is "partaken of" (*to metecho-
menon*), and the third "partakes" (*to metechon*). Associated with
these three members are a bewildering number of attributes and
further interlocking triads, all of which are beyond our needs to
consider here.[21]

Finally, the movement of any order or level of reality out of the
one above is effected by means of "analogy" or "likeness" (*Elements
of Theology*, Props. 108, 112).[22] This is an application of the general
doctrine that the relation between cause and effect is always necessarily one of "likeness" (Props. 28-29, 32, and Dodds' note to 28).
Moreover, the "distinctive property" which is imparted to each

---

[21] The reader who wishes to pursue this matter may be referred to the
following: R. Beutler, 'Proklos' *RE* 54 (1957), 214.12-62; Proclus, *Elements
of Theology* [2], ed. E. R. Dodds (Oxford, 1963), 210-212. A useful survey,
with good bibliography, of ancient thought on analogy has been provided
by G. E. R. Lloyd in his article 'Analogy in Early Greek Thought,' *Dictionary of the History of Ideas*, vol. I, ed. Ph. Wiener (New York, 1968), 60-63.
A good general account of this and other aspects of Proclus' thought can be
found in L. Rosán, *The Philosophy of Proclus* (New York, 1949). See also
the recent, and more general, survey of the whole of ancient Neoplatonism
by R. T. Wallis, *Neoplatonism* (London, 1972).

[22] It should be noted that symbolic mimesis also, although in general
contrasted with eiconic mimesis, is effected, at any given point, by a kind of
eiconic mimesis, i.e. through a relationship of direct and immediate likeness.

chain by its "originative cause" extends throughout the whole of the chain and appears, in a way appropriate to it, even in the lowest order of reality (Prop. 97).

Proclus' immediate aim in setting forth this theory of symbolic or entheastic myth is to convince us that if we apply to the Homeric myths only the standards of eiconic representation, we shall be seriously in error. Homer, according to Proclus, did not intend that we should view his stories of the gods in such a way as to suppose that behind the "copies" we perceive there lie, *simply*, corresponding models. To be sure, as we noted, there exists, on each level, an eiconic relationship, i.e. one of copy to model, even in entheastic myth. But the point is that the demonic surface of myth, while it may directly "image" or represent the lowest race of divine beings, that of demons, is nonetheless connected by ascending levels of analogy to the primal god who stands at the head of that particular chain. Demons of myth are thus not only "eikons," but also, and above all as we shall see, "symbols," proclaiming to those who are receptive a complex order of reality which stretches out behind the demonic, visible surface of the myth and awakening at the same time in the spirit of the reader a vivid desire to comprehend this reality.

The relationship between entheastic or symbolic myth and analogy is well illustrated in another passage in Proclus' essay (81.28-83.10). If, Proclus says, it is true that the two classes of myth really possess different functions,

> "We shall find no difficulty (i.e. in dealing with symbolic myths) if we refer (*anagein*) the casting down of Hephaestus from Olympus or the binding of Cronus or the castration of Uranus to our irrefutable knowledge concerning the gods. . . . If we were to say, then, to those who have attained to such visions, that the casting of He-phaestus from Olympus hints at the procession of the divine from above down to its lowest creations in the sensible world, a procession kept in movement and perfected and led by the artificer and father of the universe, that the binding of Cronus, etc. . . ., we would per-haps, in referring the fearful (*tragikon*) and fantastic elements of myth to our intellectual (*noera*) knowledge concerning the divine classes, be saying things that were well-known. For everything, which, in the sensible world (*par'hemin*), appears to us in an inferior light and as belonging to an inferior order of reality, is used by the myths, when referring to the gods, in a way which is in accordance with their superior nature or power (?).[23] For example, in the sensible

---

[23] Festugière translates this difficult passage as follows: "les mythes

world, *binding* is a form of obstruction and a check on action, whereas *there* (i.e. in the intelligible universe) it is a linking with the causes and an ineffable union. And *throwing*, here, is a violent motion caused by some agent, but among the gods it points to the generative procession and its free and relaxed presence in all things, a procession which, though it does not depart from its own source, nonetheless proceeds from it through all things in a regular way. . . . These are the things which Socrates says it is unsuitable for the young to hear, although it is proper to seek and behold in the case of those who have the power to grasp from the symbols of myth with ease, in a secret way, the truth concerning the gods." (82.2-83.10)

Related to analogy is the notion of "sympathy." To understand this, we should remind ourselves of the following. A striking development of later Neoplatonism, and one which has the highest importance for an understanding of the symbol, was the fact that the elaborate apparatus of Being discussed above was "divinized," that is, every point in this scheme was populated with some divine figure from the ancient pantheon or with at least one manifestation of the god who is the cause of the chain, and who imparts to it its "distinctive property." One consequence of this is that the divine was thought of as extending throughout the whole of reality and of manifesting itself on every level, although always in a way appropriate to that level:

"For on the one hand there is nothing to exclude these powers or hinder them from reaching all things; they do not require space at all or spatial intervals, since they transcend all things without relation and are everywhere present without admixture (prop. 98). Nor again, is the fit participant baulked of its participation; so soon as a thing is ready for communion with them, straightway they are present—not that in this moment they approached, or till then were absent, for their activity is eternally unvarying. If, then, any terrestrial thing be fit to participate in them, they are present even to it: they have filled all things with themselves, and though present more mightily to the higher principles they reveal themselves also to the intermediate orders in a manner consonant with such a station, and for the meanest orders there is a meanest mode of presence. Thus they extend downwards even to the uttermost existents; and hence it is that even in these appear reflections of the first principles, and there is sympathy between all things, the derivative pre-existing in the primal, the primal reflected in the derivative. . . ." (Proclus, *The Elements of Theology*, Prop. 140, tr. Dodds.)

l'assument, dans le cas des dieux, en rapport avec la nature précisement la meilleure et avec la plus haute qualité."

The God, then, will assume many forms as he unfolds, and in his manifestation as maximum multiplicity and materiality he will exist in the mode of divine being to which we have given the name "demonic." Nevertheless, the chain, as Proclus observes, is unbroken from highest to lowest (Prop. 125 & note).

In Proclus' words, "There is a sympathy between all things." Dodds remarks in his note to Proposition 145, "One purpose of the preceding propositions is to provide a philosophical basis for the practice of theurgy." We have seen how the various levels of reality were joined in a relationship of cause and effect which rested above all on a likeness or correspondence. A closely related notion, it seems, is that of "sympathy," in the Neoplatonic context, a bond of "shared feeling" between some object in the visible world and unseen reality. Because of this "sympathy," objects may have "receptivity" (*epitedeiotes*), i.e. "a capacity for the reception of a *synthema* or *symbolon*, a magical correspondence which links each material thing *entautha* with a particular spiritual principle or group of principle *ekei*." [24] It is through a desire for identification with this *synthema*, and through it with the cause that matter, which otherwise possesses no *energeia*, i.e. a capacity to act on its own, reverts to its originative source. [25]

With the notion of theurgy we close the circle of Proclus' discussion, and we find brought together into a single whole literature, metaphysics, and magic. For Proclus also believed that the nature or effects of certain kinds of myth were very much like those of religious or magic ritual:

> "The art, therefore, governing sacred matters distributes, in a fitting way, the whole of ritual among the gods and the attendants of the gods (i.e. the demons), in order that none of those who attend the gods eternally should be left without a share in the religious service due them. This art calls on the gods with the holiest rites and mystic symbols, and invokes the gifts of the

---

[24] Dodds, *op. cit.* (*supra*, n. 21), 222-223. On ancient ideas of 'sympathy,' the work of Karl Reinhardt, *Kosmos und Sympathie* (Munich, 1926), esp. 178-186, is still basic. In Reinhardt's view the concept of *sympatheia* was the special contribution of Posidonius, a view borne out by the recent edition of the fragments of Posidonius, L. Edelstein and I. G. Kidd, *Posidonius*, vol. 1 (Cambridge, 1972).

[25] For a discussion of theurgy see Dodds, *op. cit.* (*supra*, n. 21), Prop. 145 with note, and note to Prop. 32. Also useful are the following: E. R. Dodds, *The Greeks and the Irrational* (Berkeley, University of California, 1951), 283-311; Th. Hopfner 'Theurgie' *RE* VI, 2nd ser. (1937), 258-270.

demons through the medium of a secret sympathy by means of visible passions.[26] In the same way, the fathers of such myths as we have been discussing, having gazed on virtually the entire procession of divine reality, and being eager to connect the myths with the whole chain which proceeds from each god, made the surface images of their myths analogous to the lowest races of being which preside over lowest, material sufferings. However, what was hidden and unknown to the many they handed down to those whose passion it is to look upon being, in a form which revealed the transcendent being of the gods concealed in inaccessible places. As a consequence, although every myth is demonic on its surface, it is divine with respect to its secret doctrine."
(78.18-79.4)

"Sympathy" is the force which links the demonic to our world and makes possible our participation in it. It is also a concept which, like analogy, is employed by Proclus to suggest a kind of representational relationship differing from the "eiconic":

"(If we wish to make an appropriate criticism of symbolic poetry), let us not say, then, that myths such as these by the theologians among the Greeks do not educate to virtue, but let us rather demonstrate in what way they are not most consonant with the precepts of the sacred art; nor let us say that because of their inappropriate symbols they represent the gods in a way which bears no resemblance to them, but let us rather demonstrate in what way they fail beforehand to prepare in us some secret bond of feeling (sympatheia) which leads to a merging of our being (metousia) with the gods. Let us grant that some other kinds of myth, those that aim at the education of the young, have in them a great element of plausibility as well as decency with regard to the outlines of the story, and that they are completely free of words contrary to the nature of the gods and that they connect us to the divine by means of the similarity of their symbols.[27] There are, however, myths which are addressed to a more inspired state (hexis) of soul and join together the lowest to the highest by means of analogy alone and place the highest possible value on that universal sympathy which joins effects with the causes that give birth to them. These myths, as is natural, do not take into account the majority of men and use words in every kind of way (pantoiōs) to hint at divine reality."
(83.26-84.12)

[26] Proclus is perhaps referring to mimed representations of divine myths.
[27] There is a certain inconsistency in Proclus' use of the word 'symbol' with reference to paideutic myths. However, the passage is not unique; we should recall especially Proclus' discussion of Platonic myth in the Platonic Theology (supra, n. 16).

ications, is a complex phenomenon. For our present purpose it will be necessary to emphasize merely those aspects of the matter which figure in Proclus' theory. Although no general definition of the demonic will be universally approved, the following may come close to including those aspects essential for an understanding of the matter. An event is experienced as demonic when divine power is revealed through a supernatural *agent* (i.e. a demon) who is perceived, above all, as an intermediary or carrier of this force. This conjunction of the general, i.e. divine power, and the specific, i.e. a particular agent, is in fact already present in the earliest use of the word. For, as Nilsson points out, the word *daimon*, because it denotes above all undelimited divine potency, came to be applied to two seemingly antithetical notions. The one was that of an unspecified divine "something" which governs human life. On the other hand, because it denoted undefined divine power, *daimon* came to be applied to what Usener called *Augenblicksgötter*, sort of *ad hoc* divinities, and to other godlike beings who were often outside the pale of recognized ritual. A closely related sense of the word is well shown in a striking passage in the third book of the *Iliad* (387 ff.), where Aphrodite manifests her divine presence to Helen and compels her to follow to Paris' bedroom. "Helen went without being seen by the Trojan women, and the *daimon* (i.e. Aphrodite) led the way." (420). Here, although Aphrodite was surely reckoned among the Olympian divinities, it is her sudden, irresistible epiphany before the mortal Helen which seems, above all, to be connoted by the word *daimon*. The notion of a demonic realm intermediate between gods and men was, of course, given definitive form by Plato in his *Symposium*. There, Socrates, in his great speech, portrays the nature of Eros as demonic in precisely the sense that it is an ever-moving link between the plenitude of divine knowledge and being and human mortality and ignorance. In this special matter, the influence of the *Symposium* surely cannot be overestimated. Three later developments should also be noted. In the first place, already in the fourth century B.C. the term came to denote precisely those kinds of evil spirits to which we also apply the word demon. For Xenocrates, the philosopher of the fourth century Academy, it was the gods of Homeric myth, passionate and scandalous to a more civilized sensibility, who were so denoted. This disapproval was the product of an increasing philosophical distaste for the traditional Homeric gods and the often rather "unseemly" rituals associated with them. Secondly, the primary notion of demons as carriers of divine power was assimilated to the immensely important doctrine developed during the Hellenistic period, that of "forces" (*dynameis*). These forces were believed to permeate our universe and connect by a bond of sympathy portions of that universe which seemed, on the surface, distinct. In a characteristically syncretic fashion, demons came quite logically to be conceived of as bearers of these sympathetic forces. Finally, demons, belonging as they do to that aspect of the divine which impinges upon man's material world, were thought to be particularly susceptible to compulsion by magical tokens, whether objects or verbal incantations. As these tokens were themselves part of the chain of "sympathy," they possessed the necessary potency to invoke and subjugate demons.[29]

The preceding discussion has shown, I hope, that the achievement of Proclus and other Neoplatonists in integrating the inherited associations of the word *symbolon* into a rigorously consistent philosophical scheme was a significant one. This achievement became possible only as a result of the syncretistic expansion of the core of those doctrines which can reasonably be called Plato's own, for it is difficult to see how Plato's metaphysical universe could, of itself, have accommodated the notion of the symbolic as we see it in Proclus. In Neoplatonic speculation, correspondence, an essential feature of the symbol, is elaborated to a quite extraordinary degree. And with it came a coherent philosophical answer to one fundamental question of critical theory, i.e. how one literary feature, although only one thing, can yet suggest many other things apparently different from itself. And unity, or one-ness, figures in another way, too. For it is not just that one phenomenal detail is linked to numerous levels of intelligible reality; it is also true that unity, the source for the Neoplatonists of all being and meaning, is necessarily present in all derivative reality. The result is that, in a characteristically Neoplatonic double movement, literary details are linked "upward" to higher levels of meaning, and at the same time coherence of detail is established by a firm anchor-

---

[29] 'Demons': See the discussion, with excellent bibliography, in M. Nilsson, *Geschichte der griechischen Religion* ², vol. 2 (Munich, 1961), 200-202. 'Sympathetic forces': Nilsson, *ibid.*, 511-513 and Th. Hopfner, 'Mageia,' *RE* XIV (1930) 308.21-311.59. 'Magical tokens': Nilsson, *ibid.*, 423-4, 431 and Hopfner, *ibid.*, 313.8-314.20.

ing in transcendent unity. Also, by connecting, in a systematic way, the symbolic character of myth with the world of demons, the Neoplatonists created a striking image of the suggestive power of literature. More importantly, it seems that Proclus, in his effort to defend Homer, was led to elaborate a distinction between what later critics were to call the allegorical and the symbolical, in his own terms, the eiconic-paideutic and the symbolic-entheastic. The problem of literary unity will be discussed at length in the next chapter, but Proclus' distinction between symbol and eicon is already a sufficient indication of the place he and his Neoplatonic predecessors merit in the history of literary thought. One may hope that future scholars will view their achievements in a way that is both more generous and more just.

Appendix I

Symbolon

In view of the importance of the word *symbolon* in Proclus' system, it seems useful to sketch a history of the term in the ancient world. Two cautions, however. This account in no way aims to "cover the subject." [30] I intend, of course, to overlook no aspect essential to our immediate subject, the Neoplatonists' theory of mimesis, but the reader will have to be content with brief indications and with only one or two examples where many would have given a more accurate picture of the *extent* of the phenomenon under discussion. Secondly, the character of the present sketch is primarily lexical. That is to say, I am concerned with the *word symbolon*, and not, at least in the first instance, with the concept of the symbolic. The reason for this is a practical one, and that is that Proclus settled—and for understandable reasons—on the word *symbolon* as the term which, with few exceptions, he customarily used to express that special sort of representational relationship between visible object and unseen reality which I have been considering in the present chapter. Therefore, although I shall at times refer to those general lines of thought which led to Proclus' theory of the symbol, I am chiefly concerned with a history of the

---

[30] A reader interested to pursue the matter may be referred to the following: W. Müri, Σύμβολον (Bern, 1931); M. Schlesinger, *Geschichte des Symbols* (Berlin, 1921).

word *symbolon* with a view to isolating those elements in its meaning which account for Proclus' preferred use.

Symbolon, as its etymology suggests, originally denoted a fragment—usually a half—of a whole object, such as a die, which could later be joined with (*symballein* means 'to join') the other half in order that each of "two *xenoi* (i.e. 'guestfriends'), or any two contracting parties" might "have proof of the identity of the other." [31] There is thus present in the word, from the very outset, two notions which later proved of great importance: that, first, of a suggestive incompleteness, i.e. the condition of being a single entity which yet hints at some preexisting whole or other larger entity of which it is a part, and, secondly, the necessity of some prior knowledge regarding the significance of the whole. We may describe these as the hinting power of the symbol and its secret meaning. Needless to say, not all symbols were portions of a familiar or recognizable object. (Nor were they necessarily portions at all of some kind of whole, but could instead, like a subway token, merely stand for something else and be recognized to do so once the requisite knowledge was present.)

To what may be called the suggestive incompleteness or hinting power of the symbol and the necessity for prior knowledge for interpretation there should be added a third attribute of the symbol, and that is that its significance, and the possibility of its interpretation, frequently rest on the mechanism of correspondence. The symbol, in its original, concrete form, as we saw, reveals its meaning by the fact that one of its halves fits in with or corresponds to the other. Similarly, the symbol, let us say, of the lamb proclaims its meaning, humility, the crucified Christ, or the like, because the characteristics of a real lamb correspond to the fundamental attributes of the virtue of humility, therefore putting us in mind of that virtue, or because the lamb exhibits a meek readiness to be led to slaughter. Obviously, physical and conceptual correspondence are not the same, but they are related, and as a category they stand apart from other kinds of relationships in which one thing is indicated by another. To take one example, photographs will bring to mind the person photographed, but only because it is a

---

[31] Liddell and Scott, *Greek-English Lexicon*, New edition, revised by H. Stuart Jones (Oxford, 1940) *s.v.* 'σύμβολον.' Old, but still very useful, is the discussion of Ch. Lécrivain, 'Hospitium,' *Dictionnaire des antiquités grecques et romaines*, III, ed. Daremberg et Saglio (Paris, 1899), 294-302.

replica of that person, not because it corresponds to him in the way we have described. Nor, again, in the case of words does correspondence figure, since with the exception of onomatopoeic formations, words refer to concepts or things, not by correspondence, but in what is apparently a purely conventional way. Consequently, a painting of a lamb will clearly be experienced as different from other representations of that same lamb, when by, among other things, its non-fortuitous context (its being placed on an altar, let us say), the painting clearly proclaims that it is to be taken as something *more* than a simple likeness. And to "read" the hidden meaning of this symbol we must naturally have a prior knowledge of the concept of humility as well as some intellectual grasp of its various attributes.

This account of some aspects of the *symbolon* in its more basic forms contains a good deal that is self-evident, but I should like to justify this by observing that many important features of the later theory of the literary symbol are, as we shall see, conceptualizations of these same aspects which have been analogically extended to the problem of the interpretation of texts. Starting from this early use of *symbolon* to denote a concrete token, the next step, logically if not historically, was its metaphorical extension to those kinds of inferences in other kinds of experience which the Greeks thought similar. Thus, the watchman in the opening scene of the *Agamemnon* announces that he is watching for "*lampados to symbolon*," "the token in the form of a beacon light," i.e. the light which, for those who know its significance, is a token or symbol of the information that the Greek army was returning from Troy. Here there is no longer a question of there being two pieces which are put together and then found to correspond. But the essential fact of something incomplete or "meaningless" in itself which suggest a whole and requires previous knowledge for its comprehension is present.

Another early, and natural, extension of the term is to the mantic realm.[32] For a mentality congenial to divination, the natural and human worlds are alive with *symbola* which continually manifest themselves to us, but which also require our interpretation. Two eagles struggling in mid-air, like those in the second

---

[32] See Buffière, *op. cit.* (*supra*, n. 12), 39-41. Also helpful is Ed. Fraenkel's note on Aeschylus' *Agamemnon* 144 (Aeschylus, *Agamemnon*, ed. with a commentary by Ed. Fraenkel, 3 vols. [Oxford, 1950]).

book of the *Odyssey* (146 ff.), were probably a familiar enough sight to countrymen in ancient Greece. But when such a struggle occurred in the context of a discussion of imminent bloodshed and divine punishment earned by wicked men, and was experienced by men who regularly read *intention* into natural phenomena, it became something else—an omen or, in the terms of our discussion, a symbol. To interpret such an omen, we must somehow know the other "half," some typical human contingency, and intuit as well that what we perceive fits in or corresponds, by some natural analogy, with that unseen half. This knowledge of human possibilities, as well as a "feel" for persuasive analogies, were undoubtedly one of the chief gifts of a seer. Again, there is present here an important feature of the symbol. When Heraclitus (fr. 93) declared of the Delphic Oracle, "It neither speaks out nor conceals, but, instead, gives a sign," his words might as easily have been applied to the symbol. For this, too, even its concrete form, simultaneously hints at, and yet keeps concealed (since it is a symbol, not a likeness), that whole of which it is a part. Eagles fighting are, on the face of it, merely eagles fighting. Yet for those who are attuned to divination, the event has a secret meaning, too.

The word *symbolon* came also to play an important role in the allegorical tradition. But before we consider this matter, we should glance at the contribution of rhetorical theory to the complex of associations present in the word. In general, the allegorical and rhetorical traditions were widely divergent in their critical assumptions, but in this specific matter, as has long been recognized, certain elements of rhetorical theory contributed importantly to the technique of allegorical interpretation in its more developed stages. It appears, however, that, although words akin to *symbolon*, such as *ainigma*, which were not so significant for Proclus, were frequently enough discussed in ancient rhetorical texts, the word *symbolon* itself, so far as I have been able to determine, occurs only *once* in the ancient rhetoricians. But the occurrence of the word is in a context important for the understanding of the contribution of rhetorical theory to ancient methods of allegorical interpretation, and we may be excused for devoting more attention to it than its single occurrence might seem to merit. Demetrius, in his treatise *On Style*, examined (241-243) those stylistic elements which contribute to the general impression of power and forcefulness—what he calls *deinotes*. "Brachylogies," i.e. concise, pointed

remarks, constitute one such source, and akin to these are what
Dionysius calls *symbola* (243), subsequently defined as statements made *allegorikōs*, i.e. formulated in such a way that surface
meaning and underlying intention are at unmistakable variance.
He gives as an example the remark attributed to the tyrant Dionysius by way of threat to the Locrians, "Your cicadas will chirp
from the ground." Now, *allegoria*, the concept with which *symbolon* is explicitly linked, has, in the rhetorical tradition, a rather
general meaning and refers to an extended statement (that is, a
complex thought, something more than a single word) which is
so formulated that the speaker will *say* one thing, but *mean* another.
The potentiality such a broad concept has for extending itself in
various directions was delimited by the rhetoricians, however, in
a fairly firm way. On one side, allegory shaded off into *metaphor*
in those cases where, though the same relationship between surface
and meaning was present, only a *single* word or phrase was in
question: figure here becomes trope. And bounding it on the
other side were related *figures* of a closely similar character, such
as, for example, irony, *emphasis*, and metonymy. Now the fact
that the term *allegoria* apparently originated in the rhetorical
tradition, where it had a firm place next to such concepts as
metaphor, riddle, and irony is extremely helpful in explaining the
frequent occurrence of these latter terms in works of allegorical
interpretation. More to the point, the "rhetorical" context of the
word *symbolon*, in particular its affinity with the concept of metaphor, provides, as I hope to show later (Appendix II) a useful
insight into the origins of some important elements of Proclus'
theory of the symbol.[33]

To return to the tradition proper of the allegorical interpretation
of myths, whether these are "free-floating" or part of the fabric of
the Homeric and cosmogonic poems or the Bible, the word *symbolon*
came to be used with extraordinary frequency. Its use in this
special context is first attested, so far as I can find, in the Stoic
Cleanthes' treatise *On the Soul*. At one point, Cleanthes is arguing
against those who contend that the ruling portion of the soul
(*to hegemonikon tes psyches meros*) is situated in the head and adduces

---

[33] For a detailed presentation of the complex of figures and tropes referred
to, see H. Lausberg, *Handbuch der literarischen Rhetorik*, vol. 1 (Munich,
1960), 282 ff and 441 ff. The connections between allegorical and rhetorical
thought are briefly discussed by Pépin, *op. cit. (supra*, n. 12), 85-92.

as proof the story of Athena's birth, saying that this is a *"symbolon of the fact that the hegemonikon is located in the head."* [34] After Cleanthes, the word can be attested in this special context in a very great number of passages. What would be of greater use at this point, however, would be to show by several citations from one of the earliest authors in whom the word is abundantly attested, Philo Judaeus,[35] how *symbolon* early in its known history as a key term in allegorical interpretation already exhibited a number of specific nuances which we already observed in our discussion of the *symbolon* in its original, concrete sense, and in its extended, but non-allegorical contexts. By way of comparison, I shall cite the so-called pseudo-Heraclitus, and this for two reasons. First, Heraclitus was, as far as we can tell, approximately contemporary with Philo, and is thus also one of our earliest extant examples of a continuous allegorical interpretation of mythic texts, in this case, the *Iliad* and the *Odyssey*. Secondly, Heraclitus seems more a professional rhetorician than a serious philosophical interpreter of the myths,[36] and thus provides us, much more than Philo, with evidence for allegorical interpretation in a somewhat rhetorical milieu. We shall thus be able to supplement the rather meager evidence considered earlier in connection with the rhetorician Demetrius.

There are certain contexts of interpretation in which the word *symbolon* recurs, and which, as we shall see, the primitive associations of the word constantly reappear. A mythic text, for example, was felt to be symbolic, and the word *symbolon* or one of its derivatives applied to elements of it, where this text, due to some disquieting or paradoxical feature, seemed all but to "cry out" to the reader that it was the author's intention that the reader should

---

[34] The Greek text can be found in *Stoicorum Veterum Fragmenta*, vol. 2, ed. H. von Arnim (Leipzig, 1903), 256.14; cf. 257.32, 258.8.

[35] For a good modern discussion of Philo as allegorist, with citations of earlier literature, see: I. Christiansen, *Die Technik der allegorischen Auslegungswissenschaft bei Philon von Alexandreia*, in *Beiträge zur Geschichte der biblischen Hermeneutik*, 7 (Tübingen, 1969); J. Pépin, 'Remarques sur la théorie d'exégèse allégorique chez Philon' in *Philon d'Alexandrie* (Paris, Editions du Centre National de la Recherche Scientifique, 1967).

[36] The author of the *Homeric Problems* is misleadingly called pseudo-Heraclitus, since he nowhere pretends that he is the famous Heraclitus of Ephesus. For a discussion of this figure, see the best modern edition, that of F. Buffière, *Allégories d'Homère* (Paris, 1962). We find the same combination of rhetorical and allegorical interests in the probably contemporary Cornutus; A. D. Nock's article (*RE*, Supplbd. V [1931] 995-1005) is the best introduction.

not rest content with the surface, but should seek instead to penetrate into its inner meaning. Thus Philo, in reference to a puzzling detail in the Joseph story observes that the text "all but explicitly urges us to depart from the letter"; consequently, the detail was to be taken without question "in a symbolic manner." And the quality which above all imparts to a text that special character of "aliveness" which awakens the reader or auditor to the presence of some intention is that of the unexpected or out-of-place.[37] The assumption underlying this view is, of course, a not easily defensible one, i.e., that an author is always and everywhere reasonable, and that even where he seems not to be he has nonetheless acted with full consciousness of what he is about. It is not fully defensible, because there are many other reasons to account for the presence of puzzling features in an archaic or mythic literary text. Nonetheless, it is a common and undeniable fact of experience that a reader's way "into" a text was first opened up by an unusual detail which roused him from a too easy acceptance of the surface and invited him to more active reflection.

In Heraclitus, too, we find a similar awareness of "symbolic" contexts, not always, however, marked by the presence of the word *symbolon*. A passage (29.4) which nicely illustrates the "hinting" power of a symbolic passage is his discussion of the famous description of Strife (Eris) in Book IV of the *Iliad* (440-445). To be sure, Heraclitus' immediate emphasis is on the *obviousness* of the meaning underlying many symbolic passages, but the value of his remarks, for our own purposes, lies in his conviction that, although some passages may be easy to interpret, they nonetheless, because of some patent oddity, clearly cry out for our interpretative efforts. The allegory of Strife, Heraclitus says, requires no subtle conjecture on the part of the reader. Homer, in fact, "parades ostentatiously the various details in his description of Strife." In the same way, in his explication of the scene at the end of Book I of the *Iliad*, where Hephaestus recounts the extraordinary story of how he became lame, Heraclitus emphasizes the "reasonableness" (*eikotōs*) of the god's lameness if one keeps in mind the characteristics of human fire as contrasted with those of ethereal

---

[37] 'Letter': *Quod det. pot. insid. soleat* 6, 15. 'Out of place': *Quod deus sit immutab.* 27, 127-128. The category of the 'out of place' (*atopon*) was used in Vergilian interpretation, also; there it was rendered *absurdum*. See J. Stroux 'Zur allegorischen Deutung Virgils,' *Philologus* 86 (1931), 365.

fire (26.6). The former is incomplete, "maimed"; it needs wood to burn, as the lame man needs a staff to walk. And so, when Hephaestus, the god of human fire, is described as lame, we should not really find it surprising, for he has been so portrayed "in a symbolic way" (*symbolikōs*).

What may variously be called the ambiguous or homonymous nature of the symbol is also a feature of Philo's and Heraclitus' exegeses.[38] Here we enter into a new set of associations which it is very difficult to derive from the *symbolon* in its concrete form. A *symbolon* whose other half was *inherently* a matter of uncertainty or was susceptible of multiple interpretations would be very ineffective indeed, because it would defeat the very purpose, that of identification, for which it had been created in the first place. Whatever the explanation, this is surely from the theoretical point of view a weak feature in symbolic interpretation. It was not necessarily a "bad" assumption, but the practice did require some kind of theoretical justification if interpretation was to be absolved from the charge of sheer arbitrariness. As we shall see, what has been called the "polyvalence des symboles" eventually became the object of sustained attention on the part of later Neoplatonists, in particular, Iamblichus. In any event, the fact that a symbol might be interpreted in a variety of ways was a fact generally accepted by Philo and Heraclitus. According to the former, for example, the Cherubim with the flaming sword (*Gen* 3.24) may be taken to mean one of three different things. For Heraclitus, the scandalous story of Ares and Aphrodite conceals, in allegorical form, an account *either* of Empedoclean physics *or* of the art of the bronzesmith. In both cases no one interpretation is called more true than the other, although Philo clearly prefers the third of the interpretations he records, his own, since he refers to it as the 'more serious interpretation' (*spoudaioteros logos*).

The last feature of the symbol we shall discuss is its close connection with the concept of analogy or correspondence. This is, in fact, precisely the mechanism by which the symbol gains its suggestiveness and can generate multiple meanings. And although nothing like the fully developed Neoplatonic theory of symbolic analogy was present in Philo or Heraclitus, symbolic interpretations were repeatedly justified on the basis of analogical similarities. This was,

---

[38] For a discussion of this point, see Pépin, *op. cit.* (*supra*, n. 13), 156-158.

of course, natural, and very much the same procedure had long
been part of the ancient art of divination. Philo, for example, in
discussing the passage (*Gen.* 31.12) where Jacob sees in a dream
"the he-goats and the rams mounting upon the sheep and the
goats"; tells us that these two "leaders" of their respective herds
are "*symbola*" of the two "perfect *logoi*," the one of which "purifies
the soul of sins," while the other "nourishes it and makes it full of
successful deeds." And Jacob took them as symbols, for "lifting up
the hitherto closed eye of his mind he perceived the perfect *logoi*
which *correspond* to the he-goats and rams." [39] In the same way, in
the passage in Heraclitus we have already discussed, where the
lame Hephaestus needing a staff was identified with earthly fire
in need of fuel to burn, the interpretation rested on the perception
of an analogical similarity, which, though far-fetched, is nonetheless quite clear.

Appendix II

Symbol and Metaphor

In the preceding appendix we examined the sources of the
concept of the symbol in Neoplatonic literary theory chiefly from
the point of view of those associations which were in some sense
implicit in the nature of the *symbolon* itself. There is, I should
like to argue, another source for the distinction between symbolic
and eiconic mimesis, and that is one which derives from rhetorical
speculation on metaphor and simile. We earlier had occasion to
observe the rhetorical aspects of the matter when we noted that in
rhetorical theory *allegoria* was closely associated with metaphor, and
that *symbolon* was used, by Demetrius, to designate one kind of
"allegorical" utterance. The matter may go deeper, however, and
it appears that already in the distinction between metaphor and
simile themselves, and in technical comments on these tropes, there
lay elements of a distinction which, in some important respects,
anticipates the one we have been attempting to clarify in our
analysis of Proclus' essay. The question of influence in this matter is
a rather difficult one to pose, much less to answer. But a minimal
question capable of solution would be something like the following.

---

[39] The correspondence presumably rests on the fact that the goat was the
traditional animal of purification and the sheep the source of two substances
important to man's life, milk and wool.

"Is there some sort of fundamental similarity between metaphor and symbol, as this latter is defined by Proclus, which would make plausible a transposition of theoretical insights concerning the nature and workings of the metaphor to a theory of the symbol?"

First of all, some remarks on metaphor and its relation to allegory in ancient rhetorical theory. The chief point for our purposes is that allegory (a figure) was frequently conceived of as a sort of extended metaphor (a trope). As Quintilian expresses it, "allegoria ... fit plerumque continuatis translationibus" (8, 6, 44; cf. 9, 24, 46): "*allegoria* generally somes about through sustained metaphors." The difference is thus a quantitative one, the similarity being that both are effected through "substitution," that is, that in place of the "normal" or "expected" word or utterance, the writer has put something else which is nonetheless felt to correspond to it. Associated with this pair, metaphor and allegory, there is a group of further tropes and figures. Thus, related to metaphor we find tropes such as metonymy, synecdoche, *emphasis*, etc. And paralleling each of these are figures, which, in their turn, are related to the figure of allegory. Allegory, however, is only one cognate phenomenon. Simile is another. Now, the relation between metaphor and simile was much discussed in ancient rhetoric, and we are fortunate in having a careful monograph on the subject. Simile was universally felt to be, *in form*, an explicit metaphor. The question however, of which of the two was the "prior" form under which the other was to be subsumed was never completely settled in critical theory.[40]

With this brief account of the relationships between allegory, metaphor, and simile in mind, I should like to make a suggestion as regards one possible element of influence on Proclus' distinction between eiconic and symbolic myth. The most important aspect of this distinction, as we saw, was that it separated, at least in theory, two quite different modes of representation. The one, the eiconic, rested on a broad, one-to-one correspondence, in which the element of likeness was quite marked. In the other, the symbolic, representation was effected by means of a single point of correspondence which linked the primary surface to a number of other, increasingly "unlike" levels. What I should like to urge is that this distinction

---

[40] See the literature cited above at note 33. There is a useful recent discussion of ancient theories of metaphor by M. McCall, Jr., *Ancient Rhetorical Theories of Simile and Comparison* (Cambridge, U.S.A., 1969).

was, in part, anticipated by the closely related one between simile and metaphor. By metaphor, I above all mean that kind which Aristotle calls "proportional" metaphor. And when I speak of simile I have chiefly in mind the simile in its most extended form, i.e. the Homeric or epic simile.

Let us cite a passage from the fourth book of the *Iliad*:

> "Then Telamonian Aias smote Anthemion's son, the lusty youth Simoeisius, whom on a time his mother had born beside the banks of Simois, as she journeyed down from Ida, whither she had followed with her parents to see their flocks. For this cause they called him Simoeisius; yet paid he not back to his dear parents the recompense of his upbringing, and but brief was the span of his life, for that he was laid low by the spear of great-souled Aias. For, as he strode amid the foremost, he was smitten on the right breast beside the nipple; and clean through his shoulder went the spear of bronze, and he fell to the ground in the dust like a poplar tree that hath grown up in the bottom-land of a great marsh, smooth of stem, but from the top thereof branches grow: this hath some wainwright felled with the gleaming iron that he might bend him a felloe for a beauteous chariot, and it lieth drying by a river's banks. Even in such wise did Zeus-born Aias slay Simoeisius, son of Anthemion." (Homer, *Iliad*, IV. 473-489)[41]

The lines, one can argue, are a "way of saying" in extended form that a young man in the bloom of youth who is slain in battle and lies in the dust is like a flourishing poplar which is cut down and left to dry beside the banks of a river. It may, and often does happen, that the resemblance between the two terms of the simile extends to a number of details. Here, for example, 'lusty youth' corresponds to 'smooth of stem, but from the top thereof branches grow'; 'smitten on the right breast . . . spear of bronze,' to 'felled with the gleaming iron'; 'fell to the ground in the dust,' to 'lieth drying by the river's banks'; 'born beside the banks of Simois,' to 'hath grown up in the bottom-land of a great marsh.' The important fact is that in such similes the *two* parallel terms ("as x . . . so y"), both rather extended, are at times linked together by a number of points of correspondence. Now, if one were to suppress the correlative formulae "As . . . so," and in the part of the simile which contains the event (i.e. the young man's death) which is compared to something else describe, not some concrete event of this kind, but something in the realm of thought, then

---

[41] Homer, *Iliad*, vol. I, tr. A. T. Murray (Cambridge, U.S.A., Loeb Library, 1924 and subsequent reprints).

the other part of the simile would be not unlike what Proclus calls eiconic representation, that is, a kind of "simple allegory." In view of this it is not surprising that the term *eikon*, which Proclus used in this connection, also commonly denoted in Greek what we call 'simile.'

What Aristotle terms proportional metaphor, on the other hand, functions in markedly different way. When a shield is called "Ares' cup" (Aristotle, *Poetics*, 1457b17-34), the mechanism of correspondence is of a more complex character, since cup and shield do not, of themselves, correspond in any self-evident way. They only do so in terms of the proportion,

cup: Dionysus :: shield: Ares

In other words, they only correspond by virtue of a further, hidden correspondence, that between the gods Dionysus and Ares. In fact, as Aristotle notes, it is not even necessary to state explicitly the one term of this second correspondence, since we may indicate in some other way that we are not to take the term "cup" literally. To do this we need only assign a paradoxical, and therefore suggestive epithet, such as "wineless." A "wineless" cup, i.e. a cup which cannot be used for drinking wine, is, on the face of it, something which "calls for an explanation." It therefore immediately invites our conjecture as to its real meaning. And to arrive at this meaning we must intuit the correspondence cup:shield and the further one upon which this first depends, i.e. Dionysus:Ares. Is it not possible that in a proportional metaphor such as "wineless cup" we have the tropic (i.e. pertaining to trope) counterpart to Proclus' symbolic representation? Like symbols in this mode of representation, proportional metaphor represents not by a single but by a multiple (here double) correspondence. The mechanism, in particular as regards the vertical chains of correspondence in the Neoplatonic universe, is clearly not the same, but the arresting similarity does exist that an initial correspondence (cup:shield) has to be supported by a further correspondence (Ares:Dionysus) which is the real source of the meaning, since, as we saw, cup and shield do not *per se* correspond, but Ares and Dionysus do.

The relationship between riddle and metaphor, remarked on by Aristotle (*Rhetoric* III. 1405ª 34-37) is also illuminating. A riddle, after all, is simply an intensive metaphor, i.e. one which draws consistently upon points of comparison so far-fetched that one

cannot at first grasp the real sense of the utterance.[42] The value
of the riddle to the present discussion is that because it intensifies
certain features of the metaphor, it makes it easier for us to perceive
what might otherwise escape our notice. We had occasion to observe
in our preceding sketch of the symbol that one of its chief characteristics is what we called its hinting power. We further noted that
this was linked to the quality of "paradoxicality" or seeming
irrationality. Now, metaphor is such a common element in language
that we are likely to forget that all metaphors are, in their form at
least, irrational. To say that a man *is* a lion makes no "sense" at
all. It is only in extreme cases, however, such as our "wineless
cup" or the riddle, that we clearly perceive this essential aspect of
the metaphor. The point I want to make is that metaphor, because
of this characteristic, must obviously mean something other than
what it says (unlike a simile which says that A is only *like* B).
As a consequence, it incites us, even in its simplest forms, to
"solve the riddle" of its meaning. A man cannot *be* a lion. What,
then, we ask ourselves, is the meaning of such an utterance?

---

[42] It is worth noting that the verb *ainissomai,* meaning to 'hint at in a
riddling way,' is frequently used by the allegorical interpreters to describe
the covert intention of the writer.

CHAPTER THREE

UNITY: THE MANY AND THE ONE

1. CLASSICAL AND POST-CLASSICAL ANTECEDENTS

In the earliest known discussion of the problem of literary unity, that of Plato's *Phaedrus* (264B-E, 268D), the form prescribed for a literary composition is that of a unified whole, i.e. a whole which is also a unit.[1] The seemingly arithmetical character of Plato's formulation is probably of secondary importance, however, and we should perhaps rather emphasize its derivation from organic models.[2] Plato clearly has in mind a normal living organism in possession of all of its natural parts and with no freakish additions, parts which are, moreover, functionally related, all of them, the one to the other and to the working whole. It is in terms of this conception that Socrates singles out two faults in Lysias' speech. First, the speech, as Socrates says, "lacks a head" and thus falls short of oneness and wholeness. Moreover, it has been thrown together in a pell-mell fashion (*chuden* 264B), with no thought for an "organic" connection between the parts; it cannot therefore function as a whole, unified organism. We might compare it to a headless monster whose legs, let us imagine, have been unfunctionally attached to the middle of its back.

Aristotle, in the *Poetics*, adheres almost without change to the formal outlines of this definition of literary unity. One may note, however, that in so doing Aristotle introduces into his discussion, not unexpectedly, a further notion, that of teleology. For to the notions of "one" and "whole" he adds a third, which he designates by the term, *teleios*. This can be translated as "finished" or "perfect," but it means more precisely "having reached its final form (*telos*)." Despite Aristotle's acceptance of the formal outlines of Plato's definition, he does diverge in one essential respect. This is the criterion by which one is to determine the organic

---

[1] By this I mean a whole which is not merely a random aggregate of its parts, but something the identity or essential character of which will be impaired by the removal of any part. There is a discussion of related points at *Politicus* 284D and 286C-287B.

[2] The *Timaeus* warns us, however, that in Plato the mathematical and the organic should not be too sharply separated.

necessity for the presence of a given element in a work of literature. That is, we believe that an organism, generally speaking, needs a head. But how are we to know what, in a work of literature, does, in fact, correspond to the head of an organism? Moreover, by what criteria are we to decide whether the parts of a work of literature are functioning with each other and with the whole? What, in a word, are the conceptual counterparts in literary theory to the principles of biological organicism? It is not enough merely to assert that a work of literature is like a living organism; one must also how how we are to know when it is "alive," and when "dead" or radically "defective." To this question both Plato and Aristotle gave important answers, but, in so doing they decisively parted ways, in a manner reminiscent of what we have already seen with regard to their theories of mimesis.

What Plato understands to be the source of organic structure in a literary composition is made fairly clear by the illustrative analogy of the false physician (*Phaedrus* 268A-C). In his case, the claim is made to a *knowledge* of medicine on the basis of empirical familiarity with certain therapeutic techniques such as purging or cauterizing. A "physician" of this kind can make certain things happen to the human body, but, in the absence of a comprehensive knowledge of the science of medicine, he is at a loss to know why or when or on whom such techniques should be applied. So, too, there are poets who believe they are tragedians, because they are able to compose speeches capable of producing certain effects or states of mind in the listener. But, Plato argues, their claim, too, is unfounded, since such poets have no sense of a structured work of literature—of a whole to which the parts are "appropriate," as they are to each other (268D). In this passage and in the earlier 263D-264B, Plato suggests that in addition to the notion of appropriateness there is another concept, that of "necessity", which contributes to the creation of an organic literary structure. It is, it seemed to Plato, characteristic of an organic entity that its parts bear not only an appropriate, but also a necessary relationship to each other. The question must be pushed a bit further back, however, and at this stage Plato's answer is somewhat unclear. What, one asks, is the source of the necessity which determines which parts must be present in a work, and which parts follow which, in order to form an organic sequence or structure? The answer is not entirely certain, but some kind of answer can be deduced both from Socrates' discussion of Lysias' speech and from the analogy of the false doctor. In Lysias' speech, a necessary part was lacking, that is, a theoretical preamble of the kind we find prefacing Socrates' two speeches. Instead of taking the subject of a literary composition as something understood, an author must first, Plato argues, carefully define the subject on which he intends to discourse. But Lysias did not, and could not, because he possessed no philosophical grasp of the whole subject of Eros, about which he presumed to discourse. As a consequence of this deficiency, the parts of Lysias' speech, because they reflected no pattern of understanding in the mind of the author, were merely a chaotic and senseless aggregate. In the same way the false doctor is rejected because he possesses no sufficient general knowledge of the human body. The obvious point is that in both cases the deficiency is philosophical in character. It seems, then, that we must posit something similar behind Plato's notion of compositional appropriateness and necessity. If a doctor must possess a general knowledge of the human body and its place in nature as a whole in order to know where and when to apply certain techniques, so too the dramatic poet, it would seem, if the elements of his composition are to cohere in a necessary and appropriate way, must possess a general knowledge of what tragedy is about, and this surely includes, among other things, ethics and politics. To readers familiar with Plato this is not a surprising requirement. Indeed, the discussions of poetry in the *Republic* and of the related art of rhetoric in the *Gorgias* and elsewhere in the *Phaedrus*, clearly point to the same conclusion. Knowledge, that is philosophical knowledge—and apparently of both substantive points *and* method —*must* precede any art. If a man who has such knowledge as this turns his hand to literary composition, the parts will cohere in a necessary, appropriate and structured way.[3]

For Aristotle, too, necessity figures as a criterion, and, as well, the attenuated form of necessity, probability. His position, however, is quite different. The difference seems to be that necessity, rather

---

[3] Very much the same point is already present in the *Gorgias*; Socrates is the philosophical orator, whose special understanding of the truth allows him to create a species of oratory which is ethically and intellectually the superior of any which has yet existed. In the *Symposium* a similar conception of art underlies Socrates' praise of Agathon's *method* (199C) as well as the procedure of his own speech. That is, one must *define* first what it is one wishes to praise.

than, as with Plato, deriving its meaning from specific philosophical doctrines and methods, is instead a potentiality which is only realized in the unbroken causal connection which runs from the first to the last action of the play. An element in the play is necessary, and therefore indispensably contributes to the unity of the play, if it bears a causal relationship to what follows, precedes, or flanks it on either side. If it does not, it is not necessary and disrupts the unity of the play. Beyond this there is, of course, a further, external factor, that of the proper "function" or *ergon* of tragedy, i.e. catharsis, which dictates why necessity and probability must characterize dramatic action. For only events entirely, or preponderantly, connected in this manner seemed to Aristotle to have the power to awaken in us the emotions of pity and fear, emotions which above all require a strong sense of the reality of the action portrayed. And, needless to say, such a sense would be impossible were we not held fast by the logical and irresistible character of the tragic action. Here, too, a difference from Plato is evident. The function of tragedy has, to be sure, a separate conceptual existence; otherwise we should be unable to talk about it, but it becomes *real* only in the unfolding action of the play. It is an utterly different matter from Plato's requirement that Lysias should have a fully worked-out theory of Eros before attempting a treatment of that subject.

What distinguishes Plato's and Aristotle's views on unity is obviously similar to what we have seen in our discussion of mimesis. Here, too, one can say, at the risk of some simplification, that the distinguishing features arise above all from the respective positions of the two philosophers on the question of the immanence or transcendence of forms. As in the earlier theoretical problem, we catch a glimpse of two quite different conceptions of literary creation. From the Platonic perspective, the artist cannot achieve artistic unity, just as he cannot be "acceptably" mimetic, unless he has first apprehended, in a specifically philosophical way, the world of forms. For the Aristotelian artist, however, the ability to organize plots in such a manner as to exclude elements possessing no necessary or probable connection seems to rest on the power to perceive, intuitively or otherwise, the inherent requirements of tragic plot.[4] And even where we assume a more than

---

[4] Compare *Poetics* 8.1451a22-35: Homer as fashioner of unified epic

intuitive understanding of the needs of the genre, it is clear that there are no specific doctrines a poet would have to learn or know in order to construct unified plots. For unity, and the necessary and probable acts which create it, are determined by the special function of tragedy, and not by any extrinsic philosophical doctrines or methodological criteria.

2. UNITY IN NEOPLATONIC EXEGESIS

The Neoplatonists' conception of unity, in its fundamental assumptions, follows closely the position we have outlined for Plato. Were it not something of a circular argument, it could be urged that the similarity of Neoplatonic analysis of unity is a good piece of evidence for the correctness of the views that have been ascribed to Plato. For with the Neoplatonists it is above all the *conscious intention* of the artist, what they call the *skopos*,[5] which imparts to the various elements of his work the quality of being necessary or of belonging. In the same way, it is only a correct understanding of this intention on the part of the exegete which allows him to settle the question of unity. And for philosophers like the Neoplatonists, the intention of Homer or Plato was above all that of imparting philosophical doctrine through the medium of represented words and action.

Besides this initial, and fundamentally important, Platonic impetus, there were other factors which led to the elevation of the concept of literary unity to an important position in the Neoplatonists' critical system. First was the deepening of the inherited Platonic notion of literary organicism by the grafting on of further concepts, above all that of the artist as a creator of organisms which parallel the Great Living Thing, the Cosmos, which had been fashioned by the divine Demiurge. This model of artistic creation, with its strong emphasis on the conscious intellect of the creator, when added to the general tendency of a Platonic literary aesthetic to emphasize intention, made a conception of unity rooted in the artist's directing consciousness even more prevalent. The artist as analogue to the cosmic Demiurge, however, is a matter we shall return to in the next chapter.

---

plots. Also, 22.1459a5-8: the natural power of discerning hidden connections which lies behind the gift of forming metaphor.

[5] *Skopos* means literally, among other things, a *target* at which an archer, for example, aims. Metaphorically, it is the *goal* or *purpose* to which the writer directs his efforts.

A different but no less important source was the Neoplatonic preoccupation with the problem of unity in general. For the Neoplatonists the fundamental philosophical imperative was that of understanding how the One became the Many, or, more accurately, *was also the Many*. The relevance of this to the analysis of a literary text is, I think, obvious. If with regard to the macrocosm, in both its sensible and intelligible forms, it is the task of the philosopher to define those processes by which the One is in the Many and the Many in the One, and to perceive the telos or the Good in the light of which all things have been made, he will also, when faced with the microcosm of a literary text, be disposed to ask similar, fruitful questions. How can we refer the multiplicity of separate details in a work of literature to the single intention of the creator of that work? And what are the means and mechanisms, the processes by which that single intention is unfolded into the innumerable surface elements of the text? The relation of unity, viewed as controlling intention, to surface multiplicity—what we might call the intentional or teleological analysis of literary detail— is a paramount preoccupation of the Neoplatonic exegetes. If a work did not have oneness in this literally transcendental sense, if its details were not, all of them, rooted in the primal unity of the author's mind, it could not be intelligible or, what was for the Neoplatonists the same thing, beautiful. In the words of Hermeias, commenting on *Phaedrus* 264B:

> "Why is it necessary for the discourses to be unified? It is because in every thing the beautiful and the good desire its illumination from the One. For unless it is possessed by the One, such a thing cannot be good. So, also, beauty cannot be beautiful unless Oneness is present in all of its parts."[6]

It is the aim of the present chapter to consider the specific ways in which the Neoplatonists formulated and attempted to solve, from their own special perspectives, the critical questions created by a demand for literary unity.

------

[6] *In Phaedrum*, ed. Couvreur (Paris 1901), 231, 6-9. For parallel passages in other Neoplatonists, see L. Westerink, *Anonymous Prolegomena to Platonic Philosophy* (Amsterdam, 1962) 21 (= p. 214, 31). A useful discussion of the whole topic of the Neoplatonists' interpretation of the *Phaedrus* can be found in A. Bielmeier, *Die neuplatonischen Phaidrosinterpretationen* (= *Rhetorische Studien*, Heft. 16) (Paderborn, 1930).

Proclus, early in his commentary on the *Timaeus* (I.1.4-8), makes the following observation:

> "That the intention of Plato's *Timaeus* is to present a complete account of nature and that this intention extends to an examination of the universe, the dialogue being concerned with this from beginning to end, is, it seems to me, obvious to anyone but the most benighted. The entire dialogue, throughout its whole extent, has as its intention an exposition of nature, and has the same matters in view, whether they are on the level of copies or of their models, in the whole or in its parts."

Again, in speaking of the *Republic* (*In Rempublicam* I.11.8-13):

> "The *Republic* is about the state and about true justice. I do not mean to say, however, that there are two themes (*skopoi*) in the work. For this is not possible. If it is true that a work of literature which is of any value at all, resembles a living organism, it must have only one theme, just as every living thing is organized, with regard to its parts, according to a single principle of conformity. Rather, what I said is true in the sense that the two themes are identical with each other."

The principle that every dialogue of Plato, and by extension every work of literature "which is of any value at all," possesses one fundamental theme, *in all of its parts and on all of its levels* [7]— and only one—is a view which, as has been argued with great plausibility by Karl Praechter, was first systematically worked out by the fourth-century Neoplatonist Iamblichus.[8] According to Praechter, in an essay which aims at, among other things, a general rehabilitation of Iamblichus and the genre of philosophical commentary, there were certain serious deficiencies in the exegetical practice of the Neoplatonists, until Iamblichus, in an effort which paralleled his general systemization of Neoplatonic theology, addressed himself to the task of reorganizing methods of exegesis along more rigorous lines. Taking Porphyry, the disciple of Plotinus,

---

[7] The meaning of this formulation will become clearer as the chapter progresses. Briefly, by "parts" Proclus means the consecutive portions of a dialogue, its prologue, etc. By "levels," he means, as we do, the various levels of meaning which are supposed to lie simultaneously behind some element, or elements, of the text under examination.

[8] Praechter develops these views in an essay of the greatest importance, 'Richtungen und Schulen im Neuplatonismus' in *Genethliakon Carl Robert* (Berlin, 1910), 105-156, esp. 121-144. See also, Iamblichus Chalcidensis, *In Platonis dialogos commentariorum fragmenta*, ed. with translation and commentary by J. W. Dillon (*Philosophia antiqua*, 23 [Leiden, 1973]), pp. 54-66.

as an exemplar of the pre-Iamblichan exegete, Praechter analyzes
the short treatise, *On the Cave of the Nymphs*, and argues that
Porphyry's method suffers from several weaknesses, the most
significant of which is a failure to establish any link between
multiple interpretations of the same textual datum.[9] Instead of
citing one interpretation after the other in an arbitrary and un-
critical way, Porphyry should have settled on a single interpretation or, if he elected to retain more than one, he should then have
shown *how*, i.e. *in what kind of conceptual structure*, these varying
interpretations could cohere. The co-existence of multiple interpretations of the same textual datum, as we have already seen, was
a long-standing difficulty in symbolic interpretation. There was a
second weakness, rooted in a similar lack of philosophical rigor, and
this was the tendency of Porphyry to assign to a portion of a
Platonic dialogue a purpose out of harmony with the evident
purpose of the dialogue as a whole, in violation of what we may call,
using Proclus' formulation, a unity of "parts." Thus, Proclus
(*Tim.* I, 19.24-30) notes that Porphyry and Iamblichus differ in
their interpretation of the "prologue" of the *Timaeus* (17A-27B)
in that the former assigns to the prologue an "ethical" purpose, i.e.
one which is designed to affect the reader's character, the latter an
aim, which to Proclus' mind, is clearly in "harmony" with the
"proposed subject" of the dialogue, i.e. an exposition of physics.
If the *Timaeus* is "about" physics, Porphyry's view was obviously
an offense against the Neoplatonic demands for literary unity, a
demand well illustrated by the passage from the *Timaeus* commentary (I.1.4-8) cited above. These two faults, beyond the fact
that they reflect a similar arbitrariness and lack of rigor, seem
on the face of it not to be related in any further way. They are
both, of course, familiar questions to a literary critic. How do we
account for multiple interpretations of the same work? That is to
say, how do we explain what we perceive as its "density" or
"profundity." Then, how do we "justify" the presence in a literary
text of elements which seem to have no clear relationship to what

---

[9] We may call this a failure to establish a "unity of levels." Thus, for
Porphyry the cave is a symbol of (1) the visible cosmos (2) the intelligible
cosmos (3) invisible powers. For a defence of Porphyry, see J. Pépin, 'Porphyre, exégète d'Homère,' *Entretiens sur l'antiquité classique*, vol. XII,
Porphyre (Geneva, 1965), 231-272. There is a new and excellent text with
translation of Porphyry's treatise edited by L. Westerink and others in
Arethusa Monographs, I (Buffalo, 1969).

we understand to be the purpose of that work as a whole? Do we say that they are intrusive and "meaningless" or that the work simply has more than one purpose? Or do we seek to establish the existence of some more inclusive structure in terms of which the apparently multiple purposes can be seen to be subserving the same end? As an answer to these difficulties Iamblichus proposed a mode of exegesis which, as we shall see, offered a solution to both questions at the same time. That is to say, it is a system of exegesis which links together in one scheme the two kinds of unity: the one a unity of parts, the other a unity of levels.

Before we consider this more complex model of unity, however, it would be useful to examine an older and simpler notion of unity sometimes found in the Neoplatonists, i.e. that form of unity which does not involve a number of simultaneously coexisting levels of reality (this, as we shall see, was Iamblichus' chief innovation), but which rested rather on a simple mimetic relationship between, on the one hand, the surface elements of the text, and, on the other, that controlling conception, or conceptions, of which these elements are direct representations and by virtue of which their presence becomes necessary and, therefore, contributory to the work's unity. The distinction at issue is that between what is still a Platonic view, i.e. a dualistic distinction between the visible and intelligible worlds, and one which presupposes certain philosophical innovations associated with the mature Neoplatonism of Iamblichus. We are reminded of the earlier distinction drawn between eiconic mimesis—essentially that mode of representation prescribed by Plato for philosophical allegory—and symbolic mimesis, which rested on the metaphysical system elaborated by Proclus.[10]

The best starting place for a consideration of this simpler conception of literary unity is a short treatise, the *Anonymous Prolegomena to Platonic Philosophy*, composed, as has been argued by

---

[10] The two problems, those of unity and mimesis, are not fundamentally different; they are simply varying aspects of the same phenomenon. For those elements of a text which are one, because governed by a single conception, also bear a relationship to that conception of copy to model, i.e. a mimetic relationship. We should therefore not press the distinction between the contributions of Iamblichus and Proclus too hard. In the first place, the distinction between the respective versions of a layered universe is basically a quantitative one. Moreover, and this is the point we wish to make, if the one chose to emphasize the problem of unity and the other than of mimesis, this was chiefly a difference of perspective.

Westerink, in a 6th century Alexandrian milieu.[11] The choice is appropriate for two reasons. First, the work is an introduction to Plato's dialogues written late in the history of ancient Neoplatonism, and is a compendium of speculation on the nature of the Platonic dialogues, reflecting virtually the entire Neoplatonic tradition of exegesis. Secondly, the work is elementary and didactic, at times simple-mindedly so. In the end, of course, this is a defect, but it has the immediate virtue of stating a number of exegetical principles in quite explicit form. The portion of the work which deals with procedure for establishing the "single theme," i.e. the unity, of a Platonic dialogue is made up of chs. 21-23. There, ten "rules" (*kanones* 21.1-2) are detailed which the exegete has at his disposal in settling the question which of several themes is the *one* fundamental theme of a Platonic dialogue.[12] The ultimate dependence, perhaps evident in any case, of the discussion of literary unity on Plato's original formulation in the *Phaedrus* is made explicit by the anonymous author's citation, at the very outset, of the passage in the *Phaedrus* (237B) where Socrates, beginning his first speech, states the need for a clear philosophical understanding of the subject of one's literary effort:

> "The necessity of finding the theme follows from Plato's own words in the *Phaedrus*: 'My boy, there is only one way to plan a thing well, namely, to know what the planning is about; otherwise complete failure is inevitable.' When he himself says this, we cannot shirk the task of deciding what the subject of each of his own writings is."
> (21.2-7, tr. Westerink)

The ten rules follow. The first (21.18-28) stands apart from the following nine and is the foundation upon which they all rest. It states the inconceivability of there being more than one theme in a Platonic dialogue or, for that matter, in any "well-written piece of literature." One justification for this is the passage invariably cited in this connection (*Phaedrus* 264C), where a speech is compared to a living thing. But a distinctly Neoplatonic point is made when the possibility is denied that Plato could be so inconsistent as to "praise the deity for the very reason that it is one," [13] and then

---

[11] See Westerink, *op. cit.* (*supra*, n. 6), XLI-L.

[12] 'Rules' is perhaps a misleading formulation; they are rather questions, almost *topoi*, which the exegete puts to himself in an effort to determine which of several possible themes should be selected.

[13] See Westerink, *ad loc.* (8.21-25) for Platonic sources.

create a work of literature that was *not* one. Equally Neoplatonic, although it is based solidly on Platonic antecedents (*Timaeus*), is the teleological emphasis of the assertion that if a dialogue is like a living thing, and if every living thing "has only one purpose (*telos*), the Good (for the sake of which it has been created)," then "the dialogue must have one purpose (*telos*), that is, *one theme*."

The nine rules which follow are simply aids in insuring that the first is consistently followed; they may be divided, for the sake of an easy, though at times arbitrary, view, into three groups: those which reflect a generally desirable philosophical method; those which are the result of ethical concerns; and those which are specifically Neoplatonic in their perspectives. Under the first heading are the second and fourth rules: that the more general and comprehensive theme is to be preferred to the less (2); that the more precisely stated theme be preferred to the less (4). The "ethical" rules are the following: that the "more noble" (*kreitton*) theme be preferred to the less (5); that any theme which presupposes a personal attack on an individual be rejected (7); that the theme not be concerned with emotion (*empathous*) (8). More specifically, although not exclusively, Neoplatonic are the following: that no theme which reflects only a small section of the dialogue be preferred to one which reflects the whole (3); [14] that the theme in harmony with the explicit matter of the dialogue be preferred to one which is not (6); that mere dialectical "tools" or "instruments," e.g. the art of division (*diaeresis*) in the *Sophist*, should never be made the theme (9); that the "matter" of the dialogue, e.g. the specific characters and their attributes, should also never be made the theme of the dialogue (10).

These rules call for several remarks. In the first place it should be noted that the teleological emphasis observed in Rule 1 reappears in the third and ninth. In these, what is only a "part" or a "tool" is rejected, because parts exist for the sake of the whole, and tools are, paradigmatically, means to an end, not ends in themselves. Secondly, the author, in discussing Rule 10, speaks of the "matter" of the dialogue.[15] The term "matter" in this connection, as when we

---

[14] This differs from "rule" 2 in being an essentially quantitative idea: no mere part of a totality can contain the meaning of that totality.

[15] One may compare rules three and five, where the concept of matter also figures. In three, matter is seen as analogous to a part of a dialogue, the *whole* corresponding to form imposed by Nature. In five, very much the same analogy is made.

speak of the subject "matter" of a work of literature, has become such a commonplace that one has lost a real sense of its original force. But it needs only little reflection to perceive that the term rests on a philosophical analysis in which there is presupposed for a work of literature a structure analogous to that of reality as a whole, with its constituents of form, matter, etc. Both these elements, a teleological analysis of literature and an assumption for it of a metaphysical structure corresponding to that of reality as a whole, are noted because of their importance for understanding the philosophical bases of the exegetical rules. For the present, however, it will be convenient to do no more than make such an indication. For although both elements have several sources, the context in Neoplatonic thought in which, for the most part, they cohere most significantly is what we have called literary organicism, i.e. the belief that a work of literature is an organic microcosm, created by an intelligent artisan in the light of some preexisting aim or intention. This matter has already been touched upon at several relevant points, and will be touched on again at the end of this chapter. It is in the next chapter, however, that we shall examine the question as a whole.

The rules for exegetical procedure enunciated in the *Prolegomena*, as we noted earlier, are by no means orignal with that work, and I should like to consider several passages in earlier Neoplatonic commentaries which illustrate one of the procedures formulated in the *Prolegomena*. This is the basic requirement (21.18-28) that one theme be predicated for each dialogue, and one only. An immediate corollary of this is that one cannot assign to separate portions of a dialogue a purpose distinct from that of the remainder of the work. This demand can, in theory, affect any portion, but the problem to which it was most commonly applied was that of the precise relevance of the striking prologues which introduce many of Plato's dialogues. Two passages from Proclus will illustrate the way in which the Neoplatonists treated this question.

> "The prologues of Plato's dialogues are in harmony with their overall purposes. Plato did not create these prologues for dramatic entertainment (for such a mode of composition is far from the high-mindedness of the Philosopher). Nor do they aim at historical accuracy alone, as some have supposed. For it is not likely or even possible that Plato should have taken every detail from what had actually been said or done with a view to perfecting his dialogues. Rather, as was the view of our teachers, and as we have noted on a

sufficient number of other occasions, these prologues, too, depend on the theme of the whole dialogue. On the one hand, using real words and deeds prologues are adjusted to the theme in question, and, on the other, what is lacking in reality is filled in with a view to completing the proposed investigation. All things, simultaneously, as in a ritual, are related to the complete achievement of the matters which are being pursued. In this dialogue, too, it seems to me that Plato is advancing a doctrine to which I referred, and that in the very first words he hints at the theme of the whole dialogue."
(Proclus, *In Alcibiadem* 18.13-19.10)

Again,

"The ancient commentators held various views regarding Plato's prologues. Some did not even condescend to an examination of questions of this kind, since, according to them, true lovers of Plato's doctrines should come with previous knowledge. Others, too, although they read these prologues in no casual way, found them useful only as *outlines* of relevant matters and attempted to clarify their relationship to the subject of investigation in the following portion of the dialogues. Yet others demanded that interpreters link up the prologues, too, with the nature of reality (i.e. that transcendental world which was the *explicit* subject of the dialectical portions of a dialogue, here the *Parmenides*). It is this last group we ourselves shall follow, making our leading principle a method of interpretation which bears on the announced subject matter of the prologue. And in so doing we shall not be neglecting to attend to what is relevant. For with Plato's dialogues one must look with special care at the reality underlying the dialogue, and consider how the prologues, too, represent this in concrete images, and show that the dialogue is a single living thing, harmonious with itself in all of its parts, each fully worked out. One must adjust (one's procedure) to these facts, doing everything else of this nature which is appropriate. That the prologues are utterly alien to what follows them, as is the case with the dialogues of Heracleides of Pontus and Theophrastus, is a notion offensive to every discerning reader." [16]
(Proclus, *In Parmenidem* 658.34-659.23)

Let us turn to Iamblichus and the more complex exegetical procedure which his metaphysical innovations made possible. The model of reality which was the foundation of the more comprehensive solution of Iamblichus' was the familiar stratified view of reality which characterized later Neoplatonism. We have already met with Proclus' model in our earlier chapter on mimesis. Iamblichus' version is simpler, but it shares the two characteristics

---

[16] A still valuable discussion of the dialogic works of these two authors, in the context of the whole genre of the ancient dialogue, is R. Hirzel, *Der Dialog* (Leipzig, 1895), vol. 1, pp. 321-331 and 317 respectively.

that its levels are linked to each other analogically and that they bear the relationship, each lower stratum to its higher neighbor, of copy to model. But in contrast to the numerous levels making up the Proclan chain, the Iamblichan universe is only four-layered. This is, basically, the triad deriving from the late Plato, of Meta-physical-Physical (i.e. ideal—phenomenal) and interposed Mathema-tical, to which there was added by Iamblichus one further stratum, the Ethical, i.e. the realm in which man exists as a political and historical entity.[17]

A passage was cited earlier in which Proclus asserted, as a matter of exegetical faith, that the *Timaeus* has the "same matters" always in view, whether they manifested themselves on the level of "copies or of their models," in "the whole or in its parts." We have so far been considering only the second of these two kinds of unity—a unity of the "whole" and its "parts"—and have argued that this represents no significant departure from Plato's own notions. With regard to the second species of unity, however—that which, in addition to uniting the "whole and its parts," also binds together "copies and their models"—we shall be considering ideas which constitute, I believe, an authentic innovation in critical theory, and parallel in a quite precise fashion the transformation in the traditional understanding of mimesis brought about by Proclus' theory of the symbol.

Proclus is elucidating a difficult mathematical passage in the *Timaeus* (32A). He first (II.20.19-23.8) comments on the mathema-tical sense of the passage. Then, (23.9-16),

> "After having gained a mathematical understanding of the text,[18] we must turn to the physical doctrine. It is not appropriate that we remain on the level of mathematics, fitting our discussion to this alone, since the dialogue is concerned with physics. Nor, on the other hand, is it appropriate that we ignore such (i.e. mathematical) concepts and examine only what pertains to matter (i.e. physics). We must, instead, join the two together and constant-ly bind the physical to the mathematical in the same way that the realities themselves are bound together, and are of the same race and sisters by virtue of their procession from Intellect."

---

[17] See Praechter, *op. cit.* (*supra*, n. 8), 131-133, for an outstanding discus-sion. The Platonic sources of Iamblichus' metaphysical system are discussed by Ph. Merlan, *The Cambridge History of Later Greek and Early Medieval Philosophy*, ed. A. H. Armstrong (Cambridge, 1967), 15-19. See also Dillon, *op. cit.* (*supra*, n. 8), 26-53, and R. T. Wallis, *Neoplatonism* (London, 1972), 118-134.

[18] See Festugière on this passage, vol. 3, p. 48, n. 2.

Iamblichus is not named here, but, as Praechter has shown, a number of other passages, as well as a comparison with Porphyry, make the ascription of this method to Iamblichus a virtual certainty. A passage (on *Tim.* 32A-B) which follows immediately after the one we have just cited, is especially relevant to this point (II. 36.20-27):

> "Starting with this, let us see how the physical concepts, too, are in agreement with these (i.e. mathematical concepts). . . . The god-like Iamblichus—for it was he who especially laid claim to this method of looking at things, at a time when the other exegetes were, as it were, asleep [19] and concerned only with the mathematical aspect. . . ."

It is clear from these passages that the exegetical difficulty which prompted Iamblichus to make the fruitful connection which he did between Neoplatonic metaphysics, in general, and the specific problems of literary unity, was the intrusive presence in a Platonic text of an element which, on the face of it, had no connection with the stated theme of the dialogue. Put in its most simple form, the question is this: If the purpose of the *Timaeus* is to present an account of Nature, how are we to explain the presence of mathematical passages? [20] If we cannot do this, the work's unity will necessarily be impaired. As we saw, this was impossible, on *a priori* grounds, for a Neoplatonist to accept. Iamblichus' answer to the difficulty was direct and economical. At one stroke, by endowing a literary work with the structure of the Neoplatonic metaphysical universe, he opened the way to a solution of the crucial problem of unity. His answer was something like the following. Every level of reality is connected by analogy with every other level of reality, and whatever exists on one level has an analogical counterpart on all others. Therefore, if a passage reflecting the level of mathematical reality is found in a work which, like the *Timaeus*, deals with physics, there is no real disruption of unity, since in reality itself the physical level corresponding

---

[19] 'Asleep' is probably a reference to *Republic* 3.390B. For a more favorable view of Porphyry as a Platonic commentator, see R. Sodano, 'Porfirio commentatore di Platone,' *Entretiens sur l'antiquité classique, tome XII Porphyre* (Geneva, 1965), 195-228.

[20] This seems odd, at first, to a modern reader. We should remember, however, that for Plato there was a sharp distinction between mathematics and physics, since the former was an exact science, whereas the latter, like everything which dealt with matter, was at best approximative.

to it also necessarily always coexists, as do the metaphysical and the ethical, too.

Praechter compared Iamblichus' exploitation of such a metaphysical structure to an elevator in which the exegete can move, at any given point in the text, from one level to the other as he requires. This is apt, but another metaphor drawn from a similar source can further elucidate the matter. From the perspective of the Iamblichan system, one may compare a Platonic dialogue to a house with four stories, where there are identically aligned bays of windows on all four floors. Let us imagine that each of these floors corresponds to one level of reality and that there are, let us say, ten windows on each floor. Let us further imagine that we are looking at the house at night, that there is a separate source of illumination for each window, and, lastly, that the darkness is so profound that we are unaware of any window which is not lit. If we then imagine a house called the *Timaeus*, and look at the windows from left to right, we shall notice that eight windows, let us say, on the first floor (i.e. the level of physical reality) are illuminated. Higher on the third floor and, as it happens, directly above the blank spaces on the first floor, there are two illuminated windows (i.e. the level of mathematical reality). If we look at such a house, our first reaction will be to say that unity cannot be perceived on any floor (= level). The first floor is broken in two places, the third is barely "there," and the others, not being visible, are not taken into account at all. Iamblichus would disagree, however, and argue that the gaps on the first floor are only apparent. He would point out that it is because of a lack of light that we do not see the connections (in this example, the vertical alignments) which "bind" the floors together. He would proceed to light *all* the windows and we should see that those unlit windows on the first floor which we had not seen before are, in fact, directly "connected" with the illuminated windows on the third floor. And we should then understand what we had not understood before, that the illuminated windows on the third floor had "analogues" above and below; that is, in the Neoplatonic formulation, that they existed in the form appropriate to their own level of reality on the other floors, too.

Now, one may question the relevance of windows and levels of reality to the interpretation of literary texts. Let us remind ourselves, however, that it is most likely true, whether or not we are always conscious of the fact, that all working procedures in literary exegesis are based on *some* underlying model of reality, and that, further, any such model is in some sense both arbitrary (because others are also possible) and figurative or symbolic. There may, in fact, be no other way to talk about metaphysical reality than to construct a model, in some irreducible way still concrete, which expresses in a figurative way what the philosopher believes to be the "true" nature of that reality. In view of this, it is perhaps best to accept such constructions in a provisional fashion and see whether the proposed model is productive of some significant advance in our understanding of the process of literary creation. After all, another model we take very much for granted, the comparison of a work of art to a living organism, is on the literal face of it, at least, rather odd. However, such intuitively perceived analogues are often provocative of totally new kinds of questions. And these questions, once asked, have a way of leading the theorist into a fresh understanding of the phenomenon of literature. Just so, Iamblichus has brought out into the open an important literary question; for we have seen how the exclusive preoccupation on the part of exegetes before Iamblichus with the mathematical content of a passage in the *Timaeus* threatened to create the impression that the unity of the work was disrupted at this point. The question of literary unity leads to one final point. I am not arguing, of course, that Iamblichus' method of interpretation by multiple levels was *in itself* his discovery. Already in the first century A.D., as we saw, Philo was interpreting Biblical passages on both the literal and the allegorical levels, the latter being subdivided into further levels—the physical, the ethical and the mystical. The practice undoubtedly existed before Philo and came to be used widely by both the Rabbis and the Church Fathers. It was, in fact, the source of the familiar four-fold interpretation of medieval Christian exegesis.[21] Nonetheless, there is a very strong likelihood that Iamblichus deserves special credit in this matter, since it was he, so far as I am able to judge, who first used this exegetical procedure explicitly for the purpose of solving difficulties which arose from a theoretical demand for literary unity. And it is worth repeating that he did this by incorporating levels of interpretation already in use into conceptual structures in a far more rigorously philosophical way than had apparently been the case before.

[21] See literature cited above, n. 21, Chapter 1.

Similar to the problem of an apparently obtrusive passage on mathematics was the question, in general, of the relevance of specific narrative details to the fundamental theme of the work in which they were found.[22] Why was a given character used by Plato? Why was his place of birth mentioned? What was the precise significance of the *mise-en-scène*? Why mention that the discussion occurred at a certain person's house, or on a certain date? All this has, of course, an immediate bearing on the question of unity. If such elements—corresponding, as we saw earlier, on their microcosmic level to the "matter" of the macrocosm—cannot be plausibly related to the purpose of the work, they are extraneous and the dialogue can no longer be thought of as a unity.

What for example was the pertinence to *physics* of certain details in the introductory narrative of the *Timaeus* (17A-27B), such as, for example, that the fourth participant in the discussion was absent? Even more, what was the relevance of the "recapitulation" of the argument of the *Republic* and the story of Atlantis? Let us return to the instructive contrast between Porphyry and Iamblichus. Proclus is commenting on the words of Timaeus in reply to Socrates' opening question. Timaeus tells Socrates that the fourth participant in the discussion was prevented from coming because of a "certain weakness," "for he would not willingly have missed the discussion" (17A).

Porphyry's interpretation, as reported to Proclus, emphasizes the "ethical," i.e. human or psychological aspect of the situation: that only physical weakness will keep philosophers away from such a discussion, and that Timaeus' words reveal a kindly and devoted disposition and an eagerness to remove all suspicion attaching to his friend (18.31-19.9).

For Iamblichus, however, the "weakness" must be interpreted not only on a human level, but also on a level appropriate to the purpose of the dialogue. The "weakness" of the speaker which prevents him from attending a discussion of sensible reality is an indication on the part of Plato that the contemplation of intelligibles is superior to the study of the physical world. The speaker didn't come because he was intent on the former. He is "weak,"

---

[22] As was noted earlier, this question is best studied in the context of organicism, the subject of ch. 4. But since Iamblichus' multi-layered exegesis was used to solve precisely this kind of critical problem, it seems appropriate to study the matter in this context also.

yes, but in the sense that the philosopher in the *Republic* is too "weak" to make out the shapes in the cave when he returns from the sun.

> "Timaeus' words indicate that the missing participant was absent because he was not suited to a discussion of physics, and that he would willingly have been present if they were going to spend their time examining intelligibles. In fact, almost all the details are interpreted more politically [23] by Porphyry, who refers them to the virtues and the so-called duties. Iamblichus, on the other hand, interprets more with reference to physics.[24] For everything must be in accord with the stated purpose, and the dialogue is concerned with physics, not with ethics."
> (19.22-29)

This passage illustrates in a valuable way the single-minded determination of Iamblichus to see every detail in the light of what he conceives of as Plato's purpose. It is not yet, however, precisely what we want, since, at least in Proclus' report, it is unclear whether Iamblichus rejected Porphyry's "ethical" interpretation outright or merely insisted on the primacy of his own, but allowed Porphyry's interpretation to coexist on its own level.[25] It is thus not yet a clear enough example of the use, on the part of Iamblichus, of his metaphysical structures for the elucidation of specific narrative elements. For this we shall turn to a passage which immediately precedes (I.14.4-18.20), an exegesis of *Timaeus* 17A. The passage is, in fact, of unusual general interest, since it not only well illustrates Iamblichus' method, but also juxtaposes this method, in a most enlightening way, with other kinds of exegetical procedure. The first of these, the method of rhetorical analysis or, more accurately, characterization of style, is familiar from ancient literary criticism. The passage under discussion is the opening sentence of the dialogue, a question of Socrates concerning the whereabouts of the fourth discussant: "One, two, three—But where, Timaeus, is the fourth of those who were our guests yesterday and are today providing us with a feast?" The critic whose obser-

---

[23] By 'politically,' Proclus refers, I think, to what he usually calls 'ethically.' This is strongly suggested by the last sentence in the present passage.

[24] See Praechter, *op. cit.* (*supra*, n. 8), 129-130, and, for contrast between Porphyry and Iamblichus, 135-136.

[25] What we know of Iamblichus' method suggests the latter alternative. Also, the word '*physikoteron*,' which is a *comparative* of the adverb, implies that other levels of interpretation besides the physical were examined by Iamblichus. In this case, Porphyry's view might well have been incorporated.

vations on the style of this sentence is cited is Cassius Longinus, the teacher of Porphyry. Longinus, in familiar rhetorical fashion, remarks on the fact that the sentence is made up of three cola and that the second and third are each of them of a greater impressiveness and size than the preceding.[26] The first colon is "cheap and commonplace" because of the "slackness (*lysis*) of the style." The absence of connectives renders the style "supine." The second, by virtue of more formal links with the preceding colon and stylistic variations (i.e. the change from cardinal to ordinal), is made more "impressive." In the last, the "charm and freshness" of the words *daitymones* and *estiatores* and the trope (i.e. the transference of words denoting feasting to philosophical discourse) elevate and impart a grandeur to the whole sentence (*periodos*).

A different line of analysis is evidenced in the second portion of Proclus' discussion. We are given a summary of criticisms made of the passage by Theophrastus' "colleague," Praxiphanes, and the replies to each by Porphyry. Here there is little consideration of the stylistic aspects of the passage. Instead, Praxiphanes finds fault with Socrates' words on the ground of their psychological implausibility. The critical perspective is now one of general verisimilitude. Why, Praxiphanes asked, when it is evident to Socrates' senses how many persons are present, does he need to *count* those before him? And why, and this is perhaps the less valid criticism, is Socrates so inconsistent as to change from cardinal to ordinal in his enumeration? Porphyry, in answer to the latter point, offers two lines of defence. He argues, first, that concern with stylistic variation is characteristic of Greek writers in general; in support, Porphyry cites an exact Homeric parallel (*Iliad* 7.247). Then, attacking Praxiphanes on his own grounds, Porphyry observes, quite reasonably, that the change from cardinal to ordinal is precisely what we should expect in such a situation. It would, in fact, have been quite strange for Socrates to include the absent person in his enumeration or to have asked, "One, two, three—but where is four?" In answer to Praxiphanes' first objection, Porphyry points out that if everyone whom Socrates had expected was present, there would of course be no need to count.

---

[26] This is, of course, not the anonymous author of the treatise, *On the Sublime*. The older view that they were the same, universally abandoned since the end of the eighteenth century, has been revived by G. M. A. Grube; compare his *The Greek and Roman Critics* (London, 1965), 340-342.

This was not the case, and since Socrates was ignorant of the name of the absent party, the form of the question is natural. And effective, too, since it emphatically marks the absence of the anonymous interlocutor. Proclus notes,

> "All this, and everything like it that one might devise in an examination of the passage under discussion, is pleasant. However, we must keep in mind that the dialogue is Pythagorean, and that it is necessary to interpret it in a way appropriate to that sect." (15.22-25)

Then, following the method elaborated by Iamblichus, he attempts to show that the opening words of the *Timaeus* are relevant to its theme, and therefore not disruptive of its unity, and proceeds to do this by interpreting the opening words on three levels, one of them being the level of physical reality, because, as he later says (17.2), "the dialogue is about physics." [27] And since, as we have just seen, the dialogue is also "Pythagorean," it will be necessary to show that each of these levels bears a specifically Pythagorean stamp. Proclus' procedure is straightforward. He examines the passage from the perspective of these three levels and attempts to show how, on each, some (not always all) elements in Socrates' questions recur in forms at the same time appropriate to their own levels and analogically linked to each other. The three elements are *number*, *friendship*, and *sharing* (*koinonia*), all important in Pythagorean thought (15.26-16.20). On the *ethical* level, which is interpreted in a specifically Pythagorean way, two aspects of Socrates' questions are stressed. First the important Pythagorean virtue of *friendship:* Timaeus is addressed as friend, and Socrates, at least to Proclus' mind, is alluding to the binding nature of friendly agreements when he notes, disapprovingly, the absent fourth interlocutor, who had, it seems, promised to attend the day's discussions. Secondly, by making explicit the mutual character of the hospitality, Socrates calls to mind the great importance the Pythagoreans attached to *sharing*.

The same procedure is applied to the level of *physical* reality (16.20-17.9), save that there is no attempt to discover the corresponding form of friendship, specifically. The mention of *numbers* at the beginning of a dialogue on Pythagorean physics

---

[27] The mathematical level is omitted, presumably because the sentence under discussion, consisting primarily of numbers, is already self-evidently on that level and needs no exegesis.

is most appropriate, since for the Pythagoreans physical reality was in some way derivative of or dependent on "numbers in themselves" (i.e. "ideal" or transcendentally real numbers). And this reality bore the same relation, that of participation, to these intelligible numbers as do "numbered numbers" (i.e. concrete numbers, which have manifested themselves in the sensible world). Therefore, Socrates' enumeration, employing as it does "numbered numbers," presents us, at the very beginning of the dialogue, with an image of the physical world. Proclus continues his analysis, showing first how *sharing* also has its counterpart in physical reality. Last, he shows how all three elements also exist analogously on the level of "theological," that is, metaphysical reality. The matter need not be pursued in further detail, since the preceding examples make Proclus' method sufficiently clear.[28]

The precise relation of various narrative elements to the supposed fundamental theme of a Platonic dialogue is, of course, a question of obvious relevance to the problem of literary unity. We saw, however, that the question possessed importance in another context of Neoplatonic thought, that of literary organicism, and it is to that matter that we now turn.

---

[28] The exegetical possibilities are not completely realized. On the *ethical* level (here, the sphere of social or political experience) *numbers* are not elucidated; nor on the level of *physics* is *friendship* explained. On the *theological* level, however, all three elements are expounded.

CHAPTER FOUR

ORGANICISM: THE MICROCOSMIC ANALOGUE

1. Sources of Literary Organicism

Olympiodorus, commenting on *Alicibiades* 105C, proposes several justifications for dialogic form; of these the third rests on the notion which is the subject of the present chapter.

> "As he (i.e. Plato) says in the *Phaedrus*, 'A literary composition must resemble a living thing.' Consequently, the best constructed composition must resemble the noblest of living things. And the noblest living thing is the cosmos. Accordingly, just at the cosmos is a meadow full of all kinds of living things, so, too, a literary composition must be full of characters of every description." (56.14-18) [1]

It would be well, before proceeding, to paraphrase Olympiodorus' statement into the terms we shall be using in our own discussion. Fully explicit is the notion that a work of literature is a microcosmic organism, corresponding to the macrocosmic organism of the universe. Further (this is only implicit, but can be readily supplied from other passages), the work has been fashioned by an artisan who is himself the microcosmic analogue of the divine Demiurge. Both create with their gaze fixed on intelligible models. Now something like this latter conception had existed long before the Neoplatonists of the fifth and sixth centuries. In the first place, the sculptor much earlier than that, as we shall see, had come to be conceived of as someone who created in a manner analogous to that in which God created the universe. And not only the sculptor, for the work of the painter and the architect, too, was viewed in a similar way.[2] Again, the characterization by Plato of a work of literature as a 'living thing' led quite early to the attribution to it by later critics of qualities which were also attributed to non-literary organisms, i.e. 'form,' 'matter,' 'telos,' etc. It seems to be

---

[1] *Commentary on the First Alcibiades of Plato*, ed. L. Westerink (Amsterdam, 1956). Compare also the *Anonymous Prolegomena to Platonic Philosophy*, ed. L. Westerink (Amsterdam, 1962), 15.13-16.

[2] See Cicero *Orator* 9 (God as painter) and Philo *De Opificio Mundi* 24 (God as architect and city-planner). An excellent general discussion of this matter can be found in E. Panofsky *Idea* [2] (Berlin, 1960), Chapter 1.

true, however, that in such analyses the living work of literature so conceived was not thought of as an explicitly *microcosmic* entity. These, then, are some antecedents out of which the Neoplatonists fashioned their theory of literary organicism. We shall presently consider them in more detail, and merely note for the present that although the Neoplatonists were to take—apparently for the first time—what seems the small and simple step of articulating a theory of *literature* which rested on an analogy with macrocosmic creation, they nonetheless, in so doing, gave birth to a notion which has proved of extraordinary importance in the subsequent history of literary criticism.

In a consideration of the sources of the Neoplatonic synthesis, it is appropriate that we begin with Plato, in whose work there can be discerned three relevant strands of speculation. The first we have already considered in an earlier chapter, that is, the organic conception of literature as set forth in the *Phaedrus*. The second element was also touched upon earlier. This is the possibility, hinted at by Plato, of a *philosopher* poet or rhetorician. In a matter in which Plato is not always as clear as one would wish, the overall indications are, as we earlier argued, that as regards the rhetorician and the poet, Plato allowed that a mimetic verbal artist could, under certain conditions, fashion representations which directly imaged or reflected the world of intelligible reality and not, at some third remove, mere copies of that world.[3]

We have, then, already in Plato two ingredients of the later Neoplatonic synthesis. A work of literature as a living thing, though not yet explicitly characterized as a microcosm, and an artist who imitates directly non-sensible models. However, the third and most important contribution is that of the *Timaeus*. From this work comes what was certainly the most comprehensive statement in antiquity of the concept of the analogy between microcosm and macrocosm. In the *Timaeus* there is also a portrait, of profound imaginative impact, of the figure of the divine Demiurge, the creator who fashioned the visible cosmos after an intelligible model, and who was later to figure as the macrocosmic analogue of the divinely inspired literary artificer.

In order to facilitate our consideration of the way certain doctrines developed in the *Timaeus* were applied to Neoplatonic

---

[3] The relevant Platonic passages are discussed in ch. 2, pp. 34 ff.

literary theory, it will be useful to outline the major doctrines of
the dialogue which bear on this matter. The visible cosmos,
first of all, is a living thing created by the Demiurge; it has a soul
and an intellect, and is made by divine providence (30B). As the
cosmos is good and beautiful, it must therefore have been created
after an intelligible model (27C-29D).[4] The various species of
living things which populate the cosmos bear to it the same "species" to "genus" relationship that exists in the intelligible world
between the numerous species of "intelligible living things" and
that living thing of the "intelligible world which is fairest and in all
ways perfect," i.e. the model in the world of Forms for the visible
cosmos (30C-D). This last point is of extreme importance, since it
sets forth the philosophical basis for the micro-macrocosmic
analogy of the visible world. It is precisely because living things of
our world enjoy this species-to-genus relationship that man can be
thought of as, himself, a little world analogous to the great visible
cosmos (cf. 44D, where the human head is seen as a microcosmic
analogue to the cosmic sphere). Moreover, the cosmos is a living
thing which possesses unity in both a positive and a negative
sense, since it has been created in such a way that it neither lacks
anything (32C-33B) nor is it marked by anything superfluous
(33B-34A); its oneness is thus in no way impaired. The cosmos is a
visible shrine (*agalma*) in which the gods dwell, and by means of
which they manifest themselves to us (37C). The universe, lastly,
has been created with the intention that, as regards its details, it
should be "as like as possible to the perfect and intelligible living
thing for the purpose of representing its eternal nature" (39D-E).[5]

Two preliminary remarks are appropriate. First, it is obvious
that other literary concepts as well as the subject of our present

---

[4] On this and subsequent passages from the *Timaeus*, Cornford's comments are of the greatest value (*Plato's Cosmology* [London, 1937]). On the
particular matter of the Demiurge, there is a useful survey by W. Theiler:
'Demiurgos,' in *Reallexikon für Antike und Christentum*, 4 (1959), 694-711.

[5] Plato's *Philebus* (29) is also important as a source of microcosmic
thought. The literature on the subject is very large, but the following is a
useful recent introduction, with bibliography: G. Boas 'Macrocosm and
Microcosm,' *Dictionary of the History of Ideas*, vol. 3, ed. Ph. Wiener (New
York, 1973), 126-131. One should make the following additions to Boas'
bibliography: R. Allers, 'Microcosmos from Anaximandros to Paracelsus,'
Traditio 2 (1944), 319-409; A. Eberhardt, 'Vir Bonus Quadrato Lapidi
Comparatur,' *Harvard Theol. Rev.* 38 (1945), 177-193; F. Saxl, 'Macrocosm
and Microcosm in Medieval Pictures,' *Lectures*, vol. 1 (London, 1957), 58-72.

chapter were placed on a more profound basis by the Neoplatonic synthesis which drew upon the elements under discussion. For one thing, unity, which before the *Timaeus* had been examined in only an immediately biological context, was now seen in a cosmic one as well. It must be emphasized however that despite similarities between, for example, *Timaeus* 33B-34A and the *Phaedrus*, that is, despite the fact that many of the elements which were synthesized by the later Neoplatonists are already separately present in Plato, there seems to be no evidence in Plato's text that he transferred to a literary "living thing" all those attributes of microcosmic life which are described in the *Timaeus* or, what is the other side of the matter, that Plato explicitly wished us to conceive of the human literary artificer as analogous to the divine Demiurge.[6]

In subsequent aesthetic speculation along Platonic lines we find two developments, already noted, of these fundamental ideas which prepared the way for the Neoplatonic synthesis. One was the attribution by critics and philosophers of organic qualities, such as 'form,' 'matter,' 'soul,' etc. to a work of literature, defined by Plato in a permanently influential manner, as a living thing. Secondly, the conception of cosmic creation by a demiurge after intelligible models was extended analogically to the fashioning of works by the plastic artist. This is not to say, of course, that the analogy, *per se*, between visual artist and cosmic creator was a post-Platonic formulation. On the contrary it is already found in the pre-Socratic philosopher Empedocles (D.-K. fr. 23) and in Plato's contemporary, Xenophon (*Memorabilia*, I. iv.3-10). What is specifically at issue here is a visual artist who, like Plato's Demiurge, creates after models which exist in the intelligible world.

The latter development, which we shall examine first, was the more important one, since it seems almost certainly to have figured as the model for the Neoplatonic view that a work of literature could, at the hands of one who understood the nature of reality, be fashioned into a genuine microcosm. The idea in some-

---

[6] There are, perhaps, hints of this already in the *Sophist*. The argument of 233D-236C and 264B-268C implies an analogy, *at one remove*, between the divine maker of the natural world (265B-E) and the maker of verbal images. It is an analogy at one remove because, although both are makers, the maker of verbal images fashions copies of the natural world which has been created by the divine maker. Both stand under the larger heading of Productive Art; despite this, the analogy with the divine maker is not intended to be flattering.

thing like its final form is already clearly attested in the first
century B.C. in a passage in Cicero (*Orator* 8-10):

> "What cannot be perceived with our eyes or our ears or any
> other sense, we nonetheless comprehend with our mind and thought.
> Therefore we are able to conceive of something more beautiful
> than the statues of Phidias, than which we have seen nothing more
> perfect of their kind, or more beautiful than those paintings which
> I have mentioned. Indeed, when that artisan was making an image
> of Jupiter or Minerva, he was not looking at any person from whom
> he might derive a likeness. Rather, there resided in his mind a
> surpassing idea of beauty, and looking upon this intently he directed
> his craft and hand toward the end of rendering a likeness of that
> idea. Therefore, just as sculpture and painting there is something
> perfect and transcendent, to the mental form of which all those
> things which do not appear to our eyes are referred by the artist in
> his act of imitation, so too the idea of perfect eloquence, etc.

It has been argued by Theiler that Cicero is drawing upon his
teacher, the Platonist Antiochus, and that the conception of
artistic imitation described is only a fragment of a larger context
in which Antiochus made an explicit analogy between the sculptor
and the demiurge.[7] In any event, we do not have to wait very
long for such an analogy to be made. Seneca, in his 65th Epistle,
puts the matter in a fully explicit way:

> "To these four Plato adds a fifth cause,—the pattern which he
> himself calls the "idea"; for it is this that the artist gazed upon
> when he created the work which he had decided to carry out.
> Now it makes no difference whether he has his pattern outside
> himself, that he may direct his glance to it, or within himself,
> conceived and placed there by himself. God has within himself
> these patterns of all things, and his mind comprehends the har-
> monies and the measures of the whole totality of things which are
> to be carried out; he is filled with these shapes which Plato calls the
> "ideas,"—imperishable, unchangeable, not subject to decay.
> And therefore, though men die, humanity itself, or the idea of
> man, according to which man is moulded, lasts on, and though men
> toil and perish, it suffers no change. Accordingly, there are five
> causes, as Plato says: the material, the agent, and make-up, the
> model, and the end in view. Last comes the result of all these.
> Just as in the case of the statue,—to go back to the figure with

---

[7] W. Theiler, *Die Vorbereitung des Neuplatonismus* (Berlin, 1930), 15 ff.
Something like this idea appears already in fourth century literature;
compare Xenophon, *Memorabilia*, I.iv 2-7. Here there is only the broad
analogy between the Maker of the Cosmos and the maker of statues. See,
also, note 5 above and note 11 below.

which we began,—the material is the bronze, the agent is the artist, the make-up is the form which is adapted to the material, the model is the pattern imitated by the agent, the end in view is the purpose in the maker's mind, and, finally, the result of all these is the statue itself. The universe also, in Plato's opinion, possesses all these elements. The agent is God; the source, matter; the form, the shape and the arrangement of the visible world. The pattern is doubtless the model according to which God has made this great and most beautiful creation. The purpose is his object in so doing. Do you ask what God's purpose is? It is goodness. Plato, at any rate, says: 'What was God's reason for creating the world? God is good, and no good person is grudging of anything that is good. Therefore, God made it the best world possible.' Hand down your opinion, then, O judge; state who seems to you to say what is truest, and not who says what is absolutely true. For to do that is as far beyond our ken as truth itself. (Seneca, *Epistulae Morales*, 65.7-10) [8]

In this passage of Seneca, God is compared to a human artist, but the analogy extends in the reverse direction, too. In Dio of Prusa, the celebrated rhetorician of the end of the first century A.D., the human artist is compared to God, not God to the artist. With this we are a significant step closer to the Neoplatonists' conception of the literary artist as creator of microcosms analogous to God's great cosmos. Dio represents the sculptor Phidias as making a defence of his statue of Zeus at Olympia by arguments which clearly presuppose this micro-macrocosmic analogy. Phidias, as a *human* artist, used the most appropriate materials available, but it was not open to him to fashion his works out of "air," "fire" and the "unfailing source of water." Not even the gods can create the world of living creatures and plants, but only that "first and most perfect Demiurge, who has his needs supplied, not by the city of the Eleans, but draws his materials from all the matter of the universe" (*Oration* XII. 80-83).

As a consequence of this view, the artifact fashioned by the human demiurge came to be thought of, explicitly, as a little universe, or microcosm, a view which emerges with special clarity in a passage of Philo. In the second book (135) of his *Life of Moses*, Philo is describing the High Priest's robe, and interprets it allegorically, as a "likeness and representation of the Universe." When the High Priest wears this garment, he should strive to be worthy of

---

[8] *Epistulae Morales*, vol. 1, tr. R. M. Gummere (Cambridge, U.S.A., Loeb Library, 1917 & reprints).

it and become in this way, himself, a "little cosmos" in imitation of the robe he wears as the sign of his office.[9]

The other development, and this requires little more than simple notice, was the increasing tendency to attribute to a work of literature, once it was organically conceived, the attributes which we perceive in a real living creature. In the three hundred years after the death of Plato, there is evidence for the attribution to a literary organism of almost every feature which the Neoplatonists were later to incorporate into their own theories. We find texts which speak of the "matter" of tragedy, the "form" of a rhetorical composition, the "end" towards which a work of literature tends, and the "soul" which animates it. Unlike what we saw with the demiurgic artist, however, there is no evidence that the process rested in any *explicit* way on a micro-macrocosmic analogy; rather, it reflected a belief in a correspondence between literary and biological organisms. This *can* be a part of microcosmic-macrocosmic thought, as it was with the Neoplatonists, but it *need* not be.[10]

2. Neoplatonic Contributions

To come now to the Neoplatonic commentators themselves. We have seen the importance of doctrines set forth in the *Timaeus* and the *Phaedrus* for the Neoplatonists' theory of literature. Indeed, the Neoplatonists themselves are clear witnesses to the debt they owe these works. In Proclus' view, the *Timaeus* was one of the two works he should allow to survive if it were in his power to preserve or destroy as he saw fit. (The other was the *Chaldaean Oracles*.) His commentary on the *Timaeus*, a work of which he was especially proud, evidences by the extravagant detail of its exegesis the great importance which Proclus attached to it, an estimate which was also shared by his admired predecessor, Iamblichus. More specifically as regards literary theory, it is clearly to the

---

[9] One supposes that the analogy, precisely, is that the robe is the outer covering of the person, here equated with the spirit within, as the visible cosmos is the material image of the intelligible cosmos.

[10] 'Matter': see Polybius, 2, 16, 14, 'tragic matter'; cf. 'Longinus' *On the Sublime*, 13, 4; 43, 1. 'Form': Isocrates, *Against the Sophists* 17, and ps.-Aristotle (= Anaximenes), *Rhetorica ad Alexandrum*, ed. Fuhrmann, 28.4. 1436a24, where 'form' (*eidos*) is used to denote stylistic or 'formal' aspects of literary composition. 'End' and 'soul': see Aristotle's *Poetics*, 6.1450a22-23 (plot as 'end') and 6.1450a38 (plot as the 'soul' of tragedy).

famous concluding lines of the *Timaeus* (92C) that the author of the
Anonymous Prolegomena was alluding when he argued that the
fairest form which a literary organism can assume, i.e. the dialogue,
of necessity resembles the fairest living thing in the cosmos.[11]

The special step, then, which the Neoplatonists took in the
development of ancient organic theories of art was the definitive
transference of an already existing complex of ideas to a *literary*
artifact.[12] The consequence of this was a systematic elaboration
of the notion that a work of literature organically conceived should
also be viewed as a microcosmic organism, and, as a corollary,
its creator as a microcosmic demiurge.

> "We must now mention the reasons why Plato used this literary
> form. He chose it, we say, because the dialogue is a kind of cosmos.
> For in the same way as a dialogue has different personages, each
> speaking in character, so does the universe comprise existences of
> various nature expressing themselves in various ways; for the
> utterance of each, is according to its nature. It was in imitation,
> then, that he did this."
> (*Anon. Proleg.* 15.1-7, tr. Westerink)

The Neoplatonists, with a systematic zeal, elaborated this analogy
in the greatest possible detail. If the cosmos possesses form, matter,
etc. it must also be true that literary compositions, more particularly
those with which they were especially concerned—Plato's dialogues
—are made up of the same elements as the microcosm itself:

> "The next and fifth element to be dealt with is of how many
> elements each of Plato's dialogues is made up. As we have seen,
> then, that the dialogue is a cosmos and the cosmos a dialogue, we
> may expect to find all the components of the universe in the dialogue.
> The constituents of the universe are these: matter, form, nature
> (which unites form with matter), soul, intellect and divinity."
> (*Anon. Proleg.* 16.1-6, tr. Westerink)

In this schema what corresponds to "matter" is the material of
Plato's dialogues—the characters and the setting, i.e. the time and

---

[11] For ancient testimonia relating to this commentary see R. Beutler,
'Proklos,' *RE* 23 (1957), 191-193. Festugière, in the third volume of his
La Révélation d'Hermès Trismégiste, Le Dieu Cosmique (Paris, 1949) gives an
especially clear picture of the impact of the *Timaeus* itself on later Greek
religious and philosophical thought.

[12] The analogy between verbal and plastic artist is already present in
Plato's *Sophist* 233D-236C and *Politicus* 277A-C. We referred in note 6 of
this chapter to those passages in the *Sophist* where there is, perhaps, a germ
of the analogy between macrocosmic Demiurge and human fashioner of
verbal images.

place of the action (16.7-48); to cosmic "form," the style (*charakter*) in which the dialogue is written (17.1-15); to "nature," the manner or form of the discussion, i.e. expository, investigatory, etc. (17.16-24); to "soul," the philosophical arguments; to "intelligence," the problem under discussion; to "God," the Good, i.e. the end or purpose of the composition. In our discussion, three of these analogies will occupy our attention, i.e. those related to cosmic matter, form, and God, i.e. with characters and mise-en-scène, style, and the mind of the writer, in particular, his literary intentions.[13]

3. THE POET IN NEOPLATONIC THEORY

The last element, the writer and the purpose at which he aims, will be the first to be treated. In the Neoplatonism of the *Anonymous Prolegomena* (16.6), one of the six constituent elements of the cosmos is Divinity or Godhead (*theotes*); corresponding to this in the microcosm of Plato's dialogues is the Good (*to agathon*), which we must understand as that end or ultimate rational benefit *for the sake of which* the dialogue was written (17.31-32). We are also told elsewhere that there is an analogy between these six elements of both the dialogue and cosmos and the six "causes" recognized by the later Neoplatonists. In this scheme the cause that corresponds to the Good is the Final Cause (17.38). We have, then, the following three corresponding terms. Divinity: The Good: The Final Cause. This is, in general, familiar ground to a Platonist. One specific source of this set of correspondences is the striking passage in the *Timaeus* about the reason for the creation of the world (29D-30A):

> "Let us, then, state for what reason becoming and the universe was framed by him who framed them. He was good; and in the good no jealousy in any matter can ever arise. So, being without jealousy, he desired that all things should come as near as possible to being like himself. That this is the supremely valid principle of becoming and the order of the world, we shall most surely be right to accept from men of understanding. Desiring, then, that all things should be good and, so far as might be, nothing imperfect, the god took over all that is visible—not at rest, but in discordant and unordered motion—

---

[13] The 'form of the conversation' is analogous to cosmic nature, presumably because it is the 'purpose' of nature to impose form on matter (cf. 22.16-20). The bases of the correspondences between 'soul' and the 'philosophical arguments' and 'intelligence' and the 'problem under discussion' are set forth in 17.25-31.

and brought it from disorder into order, since he judged that order
was in every way the better.

Now it was not, nor can it ever be, permitted that the work of
the supremely good should be anything but that which is best."
(tr. Cornford)

The view, however, that the Divine *cause* of the world is the Good
or the End for the sake of which it has been created may appear
to the non-Platonist somewhat strange, since it seems more natural
to conceive of the relationship of the creator to his artifact in
terms of an *efficient cause*, i.e. that by the agency of which something comes into being. Another passage, *Timaeus* 46C-47C,
however, puts this matter in the clearest light. Plato is talking
about the creation of organs of sight and hearing and contrasts
various theories of physical causation with his own teleological
views:

"We too, then, must proceed on this principle: we must speak of
both kinds of cause, but distinguish *causes that work with intelligence
to produce what is good and desirable*, from those which, being
destitute of reason, produce their sundry effects at random and
without order.

Enough, then, of the secondary causes which have contributed
to give the eyes the power they now possess; *we must next speak of
their highest function for our benefit, for the sake of which the god has
given them to us*. Sight, then, in my judgment is the cause of the
highest benefits to us in that no word of our present discourse
about the universe could ever have been spoken, had we never
seen stars, Sun, and sky."

. . . let us speak of eyesight as the cause of this benefit, for these
ends: the god invented and gave us vision in order that we might
observe the circuits of intelligence in the heaven and profit by
them for the revolutions of our own thought, which are akin to
them, though ours be troubled and they are unperturbed, etc."
(tr. Cornford)

Here the notions of God, Good, and End viewed as final cause are
brought together in a most illuminating way. When God creates,
he creates with a perfect understanding of the Good which his
creation can bring. This Good, moreover, is that end for the sake
of which it has been created, a notion which can, of course, also
be expressed by saying that this Good, or End, is the *cause* of
the creation of anything.

There are other ways to conceive of the causes by which a
created thing, whether a literary work or the cosmos, comes into

being, but for the Platonist and the Neoplatonist alike that cause which is revered above all others is that ultimate, rational benefit for the purpose or sake of which a thing has been fashioned by God and his divine intellect. Now, it is in this way, too, that Plato imitates God, for his dialogues, like the cosmos, have a single end, i.e. the Good, and "for the sake of this they have been created" (*Anon. Proleg.* 21.20-25).[14] The immediate consequence of this for the exegesis of Plato's dialogues is that the most important critical question that can be asked is that which concerns the *end* which a dialogue is designed to serve, about the *Good* which it has been created to bring us, about—here we return to the subject of Chapter 3—that single *purpose* from which all other elements of the dialogue are derived.

That this theory of literary creation, clearly allegorical in its implications, came into being as a corollary of a firm belief in Divine Providence is a fact worth noting, since it was precisely those other two movements of antiquity sharing the same conviction, i.e. Stoicism and Christianity, which also worked with allegorical assumptions in the study of sacred texts, whether the Bible or the early poets of Greece. There is no evidence, however, so far as I know, that either Stoicism or ancient Christianity came to conceive of the *literary* artisan as analogous to the Divine Demiurge. For the Christians, at any rate, this would seem to entail doctrinally unacceptable elements.[15] For the Platonists, however, there was a part of the soul which actually participated in the divine, and when this received its full illumination, it seems that it did have the power to do something like what the Demiurge had done when he fashioned the cosmos. In this matter, the Neoplatonists may perhaps be thought of as reformulating, in their own special terms, a belief of some antiquity—that of the divine inspiration of the poet. According to this, the poet, in the act of creation, is filled with God. This is, to be precise, a different notion; to create because one is filled with God and to create as God creates are not precisely the same things. Nonetheless, they are not very far apart.

---

[14] There is another way in which the Divine figures. We are told in several passages of the *Anonymous Prolegomena to Platonic Philosophy* that Plato, in composing his dialogues, was striving to imitate God (13.13) and God's handiworks (15.6).

[15] See E. R. Dodds, *Pagan and Christian in an Age of Anxiety* (Cambridge, 1965), 74-78.

I have already referred to one important consequence of this
conception of literature: the general assumption that literature
should be read allegorically, by which I mean in a way which
primarily addresses itself to the author's intention, that purpose
for the sake of which the work was written. A significant result was
that a great measure of theoretical attention was devoted to the
mind of the literary artist himself. Obviously, it is not always
easy to separate a literary artifact from the mind which created it,
and in discussing these questions Proclus will often shift his perspective from the one to the other, but it remains true that an effort was
often made to surmise the motives or mental states out of which
Homeric and other poetry was created. Now, the final form of
these speculations would probably have surprised Plato. Yet they
were arguably in the master's tradition. For Plato, too, in several of
his dialogues,[16] had attempted to sketch what we should call a
theory of the psychology of literary creativity. In these a good
deal of attention was paid to an analysis of the psychic faculties
brought into play in literary creation, from the special points of
view both of their truth-perceiving capabilities and of their specific
sources in different parts of the artist's mind. The Neoplatonists,
too, evolved a theory of the Poet, and this, as with Plato, was an
application of their ontology and psychology to one particular
kind of human activity. In the following we shall concentrate all
but exclusively on the Neoplatonic discussion of Plato and Homer,
for although other poets, such as Hesiod, occasionally figure, they
nowhere receive a comparably extended treatment.

The unquestionable authority of Plato's writings was a given for
the Neoplatonists. Nonetheless, there was a curious double perspective as regards the question of the value and status of Plato's
dialogues relative to that of the work of the great early poets of
Greece. On the one hand, Plato's dialogues were thought to portray
a much higher level of reality than that found in the poets, in
general. On the other, Plato's dialogues, surprisingly, were deemed
to fall short of poetry such as we find in much of Homer. In Proclus' treatment of the problem of Plato and the poets these two
perspectives coexist in a rather complex way. It is perhaps best,
then, to begin, as we did in our discussion of unity, with an account
of simpler views, such as we find in the *Anonymous Prolegomena.*

---

[16] I mean above all, as is indicated by our previous discussion, the *Gorgias,*
Phaedrus, and *Republic.* To these the *Ion* should be added.

There, one chapter is devoted to the question of Plato's motives for composing dialogues. (Plato had, after all, spoken slightingly of written compositions in the *Phaedrus*.) The Neoplatonists' chief answer, i.e. Plato's desire to assimilate himself to God, we have already considered. Other reasons, however, such as the desire to teach and to reform are also hinted at (*Anon. Proleg.* 14.19-21, 15.20-50). In this discussion of Plato as author, there is never a hint that Plato is not superior to the poets; they create with *mania*, he with *logos* (7.15-33).[17]

In the commentaries of Proclus, however, the matter is treated in a much more complex way. The basis of Proclus' treatment is his theory of the three states (*hexeis*) of the soul and of the three modes of poetic composition which are the product of each. The belief that Plato posited three psychic states and a corresponding number of species of poetic composition, and that these same divisions were already explicitly in evidence in Homer, is argued at length by Proclus in Chs. 5-7 of the second book of the longer of his two essays. The first of these chapters (5) consists of the *a priori* assertion, quite independently of any textual support from either Plato or Homer, of the reality of these three states of soul. The first, the "best and most perfect" "life" (*zoe*) of the soul, is that in which union with the divine is achieved; it is a state in which the soul "transcends its own intellect" (*nous*) (177.15-23). The analogous form of poetry (178.10-179.3), the *entheastic* (cf. 179.3), "places the soul in the very causes of reality, bringing, by virtue of an indescribable union, that which is filled into identity with what fills, etc." i.e. it annihilates those oppositions in terms of which intellect (*nous*) necessarily perceives reality. Alluding to *Phaedrus* (244D) Proclus calls it a "madness superior to everyday common sense."[18]

The intermediate state of soul (177.23-178.2), "second in dignity and power," is that of intellect and scientific understanding (*nous* and *episteme*); a "reversion" from the "god-filled life" of

---

[17] There is a curious inconsistency, since Homer is paid the compliment of being described as a poet of inexhaustible meaning (1.35-36). In this work Plato is commonly designated as 'god-like' (*theios*), an epithet elsewhere commonly applied to Homer.

[18] There are elements in the description of entheastic poetry which find no correspondence in Proclus' discussion of the other poetic species. For example, Proclus tells us (178.26-179.3) that the "existence" (*hyparxis*) of the divine to which entheastic poetry leads us is 'proportion' (*symmetria*). For that reason, even this poetry, on its lowest levels, is "adorned" with meter and rhythm.

the soul, it "unfolds the multiplicity of *logoi* and contemplates the multiform transformation of the ideas." [19] Its species of poetry (179.3-15) *"knows* the being of reality" (rather than *experiencing* it directly by union) and "delights in contemplating noble acts and words." All of this it expresses in poetic form, creating the kind of poems which are valued by the wise for their good counsel, their power of communicating virtue, and the remembrance they bring the soul of its destiny and powers.

Lowest of all is that state (178.2-5) in which the soul is filled with mere sensuous "images and perceptions." Its corresponding species of poetry (179.15-32) is "intermingled with opinions and images, is filled with mere copying *(mimesis)*, and is, and is said (by Plato in *Rep.* X), to be nothing but representational *(mimetike)."* It is mired in the phenomenal world, exploiting its sounds and images for the sole purpose of charming the soul. It is "an illusionistic sketch *(skiagraphia)* of reality, not an accurate knowledge of it." Unlike the other two modes of poetry, it has sub-species, two in number: the one *(to eikastikon)*, aims at a representation of reality as it *exists objectively*; the other *(to phantastikon)*, at a representation of phenomenal reality as it *appears* to the viewer.[20]

Proclus goes on to argue that in both Plato and Homer we find evidence of this three-fold division of the soul and of poetry. The precise details of Proclus' lengthy discussion need not be rehearsed here. Its chief importance is that it will allow us to clarify the matter of which we spoke earlier, the ambiguous nature of Proclus' view of Plato's value relative to the poets. Proclus would undoubtedly have endorsed the assertion of the author of the *Anonymous Prolgeomena* that Plato was superior to the poets,[21] but he would have done so only so long as it was understood that one was speaking of those poets creating within the lowest form of poetry. But once

---

[19] There is a curious conflation of two faculties, *nous* and *episteme*, usually kept distinct in Neoplatonic thought. The former term, *nous*, customarily denotes that part of the human mind which perceives the object of its contemplation intuitively, all at once, without step-by-step analysis. It is the latter activity which is regularly associated with *episteme*. Proclus clearly wishes to curtail a four-part analysis of mental activity in order to accommodate it to his tripartite scheme of poetic faculties.

[20] This is a reference to a passage in the *Sophist* (235D-236C).

[21] He would, however, have disagreed with the reason, which involved, as we saw, a depreciation of 'madness' *(mania)*. Proclus clearly believed that the inspired unification of the philosopher with the One was a species of madness to be revered.

these are left behind, the fact is that, in Proclus' view, Plato *as
writer* was, at best, only the equal of the middle rank of poets;
and, in comparison with the highest form of poetic composition,
the "god-filled" or entheastic," he was distinctly inferior. This
is made clear in the two chapters of Proclus' essay where he discusses
Plato as a writer. In the first (I.2), it is Plato's particular activity
as a writer of myths that is singled out; there he is viewed, by
implication, as a rival creator of the poets.[22] In the second (II.3),
in a manner reminiscent of one defender of Homer against Plato's
strictures, Proclus endeavors to show that Plato is an imitator
(*zelotes*) of Homer with respect to his style, plot structures, and,
what seems curious to us, his doctrines.

In the earlier of these two chapters, that in Book I, Plato is
characterized as a great creator of educational myths (73.16-30),
i.e. myths of the sort which, as we saw, were recommended by
those who failed to understand symbolic poetry as embodying the
most appropriate form for the representation of divine realities.
Now it is evident from even a brief glance at Proclus' description
of Plato's myths that there is no essential difference between the
characteristics of Plato's mythic composition and the middle
range of poetry we have just now examined; both are didactically
inspired narratives and both are based on a correct philosophical
understanding of the world of human ethics and of the destiny
and nature of the soul.[23] As an example we may cite the characterization of Platonic myth which occurs in a passage in the second
chapter of the first book (73.16-23):

> "Plato himself often instructs us through the medium of images
> on divine matters in the way of the mysteries, and no shamefulness
> nor suggestion of disorder nor turbulent and material semblances
> find their way into his myths. Rather, his thoughts are hidden,

---

[22] I think it is important to distinguish Plato's activity as a writer from
that as a thinker, since there could have been no question for the Neoplatonists that Plato, in his own contemplative experience, had achieved union
with the One. As we saw in ch. 2, n. 16, there was, in fact, some uncertainty
in Proclus' mind on this fundamental matter: Plato's myths are described in
the *Platonic Theology* as works of a *symbolic* nature.

[23] The situation is somewhat different in Proclus' earlier essay, *Plato's
Opinions on Poetry, etc. (In Rempublicam*, ed. Kroll, vol. I, 42-69). There
the poet, despite foreshadowings of Proclus' more developed views (e.g.
57.23-58.27), is characterized as working in the *paideutic* mode, which, as we
have argued, corresponds to the *middle* species of poetry. This is made
especially clear by 65.16-67.9.

undefiled; and placed before them, like visible statues made in the likeness of things within them, are likenesses of his secret teaching."

After stating his view that Plato's myths represent, as literature, a form of artistic imitation inferior to what he terms entheastic or symbolic poetry, Proclus makes a rather more surprising assertion in ch. 3 of Book II. One purpose of Proclus' essay was apologetic. It was his aim to defend Homer—not against Plato, as did the author of the *Homeric Problems*, for this would imply real hostility on Plato's part—but rather against those who, Proclus believed, misunderstood what Plato really thought and exploited him for their own polemical ends. Proclus' defence of Homeric poetry is a complex matter, but one tactic he employed was to attempt to demonstrate that Plato, as a writer, was a follower of Homer in *all* aspects of his literary composition, i.e. as regards both style *and* subject matter (II.3).[24] The assertion that Plato derived his inspiration and "stole" his subject matter from Homer is not surprising in a hostile critic of Plato, but it seems, in a way, extra-ordinary for a Platonist.[25] The question of how such a belief could have come about is not an easy one to settle. But two points can be made. First, we should remember that the emphasis is exclusively on Plato's written works, and these, as regards the form of imitation which they employ, nowhere rise to what Proclus would judge to be symbolic or entheastic modes of representation, such as are found in the Homeric myths. At their highest they exemplify the form of literature which Proclus associates with the working of the Intellect; this gives us, at best, only the Intellect's view of the world of ideas, human conduct, and the nature of the soul. It is not the work of inspired, symbolic unifying, although, to be sure, Proclus must certainly have believed that Plato was capable of that experience of union with the divine which is the source of entheastic poetry.

Secondly, as regards the actual doctrines (as opposed to the form in which they are communicated) which, according to Proclus, Plato derived from Homer, we should remember that for whatever reasons antiquity, and particularly late antiquity, was sympathetic

---

[24] A crucial argument based on this "fact" is that it would be an ungrate-ful and inconsistent, and therefore inherently inconceivable, act on Plato's part to condemn the very man who was the source of all that was most valuable in his own works.

[25] The charge of "plagiarism" was an important tactic of Ps.-Heraclitus, the author of the *Homeric Problems*. See, especially, chs. 4, 76-78.

to the belief that human wisdom was revealed in a definitive way at the beginning of civilization, and that it was, in later ages, progressively obscured, only to be rediscovered at certain rare intervals by men of great genius. Proclus clearly thought of Plato as one such man, standing to Homer in the relation of inspired student to primal source of wisdom.[26] As Proclus says at one point, Plato took over from Homer "all of his doctrines concerning nature" and used his philosophical genius to "bind them fast successfully with the bonds of irrefutable proofs" (172.6-9, cf. 158.16-159.6).

In any event, it is a fact that Proclus, in the third chapter of Book II, argues for an extraordinary degree of dependence on Homer on the part of Plato. From Homer Plato derives his gift for representing characters in a remarkably life-like way (163.19-164.7). From him he also derives a number of his most important doctrines (164.8-170.26). (Needless to say, this "identity" of doctrine is established by the Neoplatonists' own exegeses of the Homeric and Platonic passages in question.) Lastly, even some of Plato's plot-structures are derived from Homer (170.27-171.10). Thus, Proclus discerns in the three-fold repetition of the argument of the *Republic*, i.e. as it first "really" happened in the Peiraeus, as it is retold the next day in the city (i.e. in the text of the *Republic*), and as it is "recapitulated" in the beginning of the *Timaeus*, an imitation of Homer's technique in the *Odyssey*. For there, too, Odysseus "experienced" the actual adventures, relates them to the Phaeacians, and then, finally, recounts them briefly to Penelope.[27]

---

[26] On this matter one should consult, above all, F. Buffière, *Les mythes d'Homère et la pensée grecque* (Paris, 1956).

[27] One must hesitate to reject such views entirely out of hand. To take a clear example, it would be hard to deny that the eschatological myths of the *Phaedo, Gorgias* and *Republic* did not depend, in some way, on Book II of the *Odyssey*, the account of Odysseus' descent into the underworld. In a broader sense, as was argued in Cornford's pioneering work, *From Religion to Philosophy* (London, 1912), one can best understand early Greek philosophy, not as a rejection of earlier myth, but as a transposition of fundamental categories of myth into a new language. From such a perspective, the question of Homer's influence on Plato cannot be so easily dismissed as far-fetched or pointless. Certainly, one ancient critic, "Longinus," did not hesitate to speak of Plato as a writer who "more than any other, chanelled to himself a multitude of streams from the Homeric source" (13.3). One should also consult Cornford's later work, *Principium Sapientiae* (Cambridge, 1952).

Homer, then, at the source, and Plato drawing upon his inexhaustibly inspired poetry. It is this conviction, at once traditional and deeply felt, which is the moving force of the Neoplatonists' defence of poetry. From such a perspective, it was unthinkable to Proclus that Homer could really be what Plato appeared to say that he was. It was therefore unthinkable that Plato really could mean what some interpreters argued that he did mean. It is no exaggeration to say that for the Neoplatonists there were two Gods, Homer and Plato, and that there was very much the same urgent necessity to reconcile the two as the Christians felt in the face of contradictions between the Old and the New Testaments. There is a passage which gives evidence of the genuine anguish on the part of the Neoplatonists when they were forced to deal with a passage in which their Master attacked the poets. Proclus relates a story concerning the Platonist Origen which he found in Porphyry's commentary on the *Timaeus*. This unfortunate follower of Plato "roared and strained and sweated for three days" as a consequence of the remarks Socrates makes at *Timaeus* 19D-E about the inadequacy of the poets to portray more than the narrow range of their immediate surroundings and their consequent inability to portray the victorious primeval Athens. To Origen the problem seemed formidable, and he "endeavored to show that Homer's poetic art was equal to the task of portraying virtuous actions. Who was more magniloquent than Homer? For he, when he brought the gods together in strife and battle, did not fail in his portrayal, but spoke sublimely in a way adequate to the nature of his subject." [28]

Very much the same dismay is evident in the opening portion of Proclus' essay:

> "Recently, as I was lecturing at a celebration of Plato's birthday, the idea came to me of considering how one might frame suitable arguments in answer to Socrates in the *Republic* by showing how Homer's doctrines concerning matters human and divine were in complete accord with both the nature of reality and the most important doctrines of the Philosopher himself. I also thought to consider how one might free Plato from (seeming) internal contradictions and show that everything he says by way of praise or blame for Homer derives from a single science, a single intellectual enquiry, a single divine plan. For once one has looked at this matter,

---

[28] Compare Hermeias on *Phaedrus* 247B (*In Phaedrum*, ed. Couvreur, 146.25-147.6).

one may well raise the following difficulty. If Plato correctly set out to refute Homer and show that he is out of harmony with the truth concerning reality, how is it still possible to include this poet among those who possess true knowledge, true knowledge, moreover, of doctrines concerning the divine races and eternal beings? But if, on the other hand, these and other matters as well have been deemed worthy by Homer of a suitable treatment (*paradosis*), how can we still allow that Plato is acting intelligently and with irrefutable knowledge? The situation in any case is as I have described, and needs investigation. I think that what most of all requires lengthy examination is the fact that Plato himself is self-contradictory in what he says about Homer. For how can there be any agreement between the "divine poet" of the *Phaedo* (95A) and the poet of the *Republic* (X. 597E), who is shown to be at three removes from the truth?

"Come, then, let us bring together everything we heard from our teacher (i.e. Syrianus) [29] when he discussed these matters and argued for the doctrinal agreement which exists between the Homeric poems and the truth perceived by Plato at a later period. Let us then proceed in a detailed way and examine, first of all, whether it is possible to resolve the objections of Socrates (Book I of Proclus' essay); second, to discover the purpose of this apparent opposition to Homer (Book II); third, to show that what Plato has set forth in all his writings concerning the art of poetry itself, and Homer, constitutes one, irrefutable truth (Book II). For in this way both Homer and Plato may be revealed to us as contemplating the divine world with understanding and knowledge, to be teaching, both of them, the same doctrines about identical matters, to have proceeded from one God and to be participating in the same chain of being, both of them expounders of the same truth concerning reality."
(Proclus *In Rempublicam* I.69.23-70.21, 71.2-17)

How did the Neoplatonists resolve these difficulties? As is clear from Proclus' remarks, there were felt to be two distinct necessities which the apologist of Homer faced. First, to show that the doctrines which Homer taught, under the veil of symbols to be sure, were not only in consonance with reality itself, but with Platonic philosophy. The latter part of this point is, of course, necessarily implied by the former. Proclus' chief strategy was to argue for the existence in Homer's poems of entheastic or symbolic modes of poetry, which he went on to discuss at great length in the next chapter of Book I. Proclus' conclusions, which we discussed in chapter 2, are intended to provide the theoretical foundation of the symbolic

---

[29] A good account of Syrianus will be found in the following: K. Praechter 'Syrianos' *RE* 4, 2nd ser. (1932), 1728-1775.

readings of those episodes which Socrates had singled out for criticism in *Republic* I-III. And, as the Homeric passages were inevitably discovered to be symbolic representations of Neoplatonic doctrines and these, one should remember, the Neoplatonists believed to be authentic Platonic doctrine—Proclus was able, in Book I of his essay, to answer the first of the difficulties enunciated above, i.e. to "resolve the objections of Socrates."

However, the second difficulty remains. How can we save Plato from the charge of inconsistency? For although his attacks on poetry and on Homer were clearly enough stated, it seemed equally clear to Proclus that Plato on a number of occasions "exalted Homer as a guide to all truth." [30] Now, Proclus' method in answering this difficulty is a trifle more complex than his procedure in Book I. There he merely stated a theory of poetry and then proceeded to show that in terms of it Homer's poems could be shown to contain precisely those doctrines which are also found in Plato. In all this there is relatively little explicit attention to Plato's theory of poetry. But now, although Proclus will continue to use his theory of entheastic poetry as the foundation of his defence of Homer, he will also be compelled to come to some sort of terms with Plato's view on Homer and on poetry in general. Opinions as to his success or intellectual responsibility will necessarily depend on the views we ourselves take of any given Platonic passage under discussion. One remark, however, may be made by way of anticipation as well as of mitigation, and that is that although Proclus, in endeavoring to free Plato from the charge of contradiction, is often guilty of evident misinterpretations, he nonetheless repeatedly found it possible, as we shall see, to make certain assertions only because of ambiguities in Plato's own views on poetry. If Proclus is often able to make Plato say something he most likely never intended, it is sometimes because Plato himself treated the subject of poetry with so many qualifications, both ironic and otherwise. In any event, the problem for Proclus was to show what Plato meant when he appeared to be condemning Homer out of hand. For it was an article of faith that Plato could never seriously have meant to do so.

Proclus' attempt to solve the "Homeric Question" takes up the whole of Book II. Despite some repetitions, obscurities, and simple

---

[30] The first chapter of the second book of Proclus' essay is devoted to proving this point (145.14-159.6).

contradictions, the ten chapters of Book II are a well-organized attempt to come to terms with the difficulties concerning Homer and poetry in general which Plato raised in a number of his dialogues. Proclus' exposition takes the form of a series of general claims advanced by himself, which are then countered by objections suggested by Platonic texts, and followed, in the same chapter, by answers to these objections. A tabular analysis will help to make this clear:

Claim I (ch. 1): Plato clearly proclaims Homer a "Guide to All Truth"

Objection I (ch. 2): Then why does Plato say Homer is unsuited to the youth of the Ideal Republic?

Supporting Disgressions:

    A. (ch. 3): Plato is an imitator of Homer.

    B. (ch. 4): Answer to a difficulty posed by a passage in the *Phaedrus*.

Claim II (chs. 5-7): There exists a hierarchy of three forms of poetry.

Objection II (ch. 8): If Homer is an example of the highest form of poetry, why is he expelled in Book X?

Claim III (ch. 9): Homer is an educator and statesman.

Objection III (ch. 10): Then why does Plato say he is not?

In my subsequent discussion, I do not intend to pass judgment on the validity, i.e. the accuracy as interpretations of Plato's text, of the three major claims which Proclus will make. He is certain that Plato saw in Homer an inspired source of wisdom, and that Plato also believed in the existence of entheastic poetry. Now, Plato, although he undoubtedly did believe that the poets were sometimes divinely inspired, was nonetheless, as we saw in Chapter 2, clearly skeptical about the value of their revelations to the philosophers. Moreover, there is obviously no trace at all in Plato's dialogues of a belief in what Proclus calls entheastic or symbolic poetry, since this conception rests on metaphysical notions elaborated long after Plato's own time.

What, then, is the basis of Proclus' attempt to mitigate Plato's condemnation of Homer and the poets? Put in the broadest possible way, it is the systematic assertion that Plato's objections are everywhere *qualified objections*. It is never the case, according to Proclus, that Plato rejects the poets *per se*, but rather that he rejects them as inappropriate to certain educational contexts or "psychological" states. That this is the case as regards Plato seems indisputably true in some way. It is also, unfortunately, an undeniable fact that Proclus has radically misinterpreted the substance of Plato's qualifications. Plato's position we shall consider shortly. Let us first turn our attention to Proclus.

In the second chapter of Book II Proclus endeavors to answer the objection that if Plato did honour Homer as a "guide to all truth," it is strange that he should have rejected him as "unsuitable for the young." Proclus' answer, in its essentials, is that Homer's poetry, being symbolic and thus necessarily immersed, on its lowest or "demonic" level, in the phenomenal world, the region of maximum multiplicity, cannot be thought of as in any way appropriate to, i.e. of like nature to, the young of the ideal state. For these only one mode of existence is ordained, that of undeviating simplicity and uniformity:

> "For it can never happen that the variegated will be brought into harmony with the simple, the multiform with the uniform, or the imitative class (*genos*) with the model of the best life. We are sketching, as Socrates says, a model of a correct and perfect state (*Republic* V. 472C-D). That is why, with an eye to exactitude, we attribute all that is good to it—unification, simplicity, truth, self-sufficiency. And so, if one were to assign shape, dimension and color to those intelligible forms which we posit as models of reality, or should add anything else which is appropriate to the copies (*eikones*) of these forms, but not to the primary and truly existing classes (*gene*), we assert that such a man is confounding things distinct in their being and weaving together separate threads. In the same way, I think, we shall never permit that to natures born and nurtured in the most perfect state and brought to perfection according to the model of the best education there be offered verbal representations and forms (*eide*) of every kind of life and dramatic portrayals of the various passions found among men." (I.162.3-19)

And,

> "If it is true that in the case of those who are being raised by the lawgiver himself and brought to perfection according to the primal (*protiston*) form of life and obliged both to keep their souls pure of all multiplicity and a disposition contrary to the beautiful and the good and to look only upon the 'definition' (*horos*) of virtue (i.e. the Form of virtue), if it is true, then, that in the case of these young people instruction of such a kind (i.e. Homeric poetry) is unsuitable, because in this poetry there have been fashioned varied screens to be set before the simplicity of divine things and

there have been made out of repulsive words and deeds and things contrary to nature veils to be placed before the transcendent truth of these divine matters and the substance which lies beyond all beautiful things, how is it right, in view of all this, to deny Homer's doctrines to Plato's philosophy, unless we are also willing to keep separate Plato's own activity (as a writer) from his activity as a philosopher? (159.10-22) [31]

It is thus the inescapable rootedness of symbolic poetry in the realm of phenomenal diversity which makes it inappropriate for the young of the ideal state. For this state, as Proclus points out, is an ideal "model," and it is only from this that Plato wishes to exclude Homer, as in fact he necessarily must if symbolic poetry possesses the characteristics which Proclus attributes to it and Homer is a symbolic poet. It is interesting to note that in our earlier discussion of mimesis the reason we saw for Proclus' exclusion of Homeric poetry was quite different and was directed at criticisms Socrates made in the context of a reformed, not ideal state. There, Proclus argued (Book I, ch. 2) that the reason that the young should not read Homer was that they were not advanced enough to comprehend symbolic poetry.

In chapter 8, Proclus gives us his reply to a second objection, overlapping with the first, but differently focused. If, as Proclus has just argued in the preceding three chapters, entheastic poetry exists, and Homer is an entheastic poet, and, as well, Plato knew this,[32] one is forced to ask why Plato seemingly condemned poetry in so all-inclusive a way in the Tenth Book of the *Republic*. Proclus' answer is ingenious, although blatantly circular. Plato, Proclus says, rejected poetry only "in so far as it is mimetic" (*Rep.* X 595A). The term "mimetic" is then restricted to what Proclus had previously called "phantastic" poetry, which, as we saw, was the lower sub-species of the lowest of the three forms of poetry. But, says Proclus, if Homer is, as we have proven he is, an entheastic poet and the source of Plato's art and wisdom, it is unthinkable that Homer, too, is to be included in Plato's category of the mimetic:

---

[31] The point of the concluding remark of this obscure passage is apparently that, *as writers*, Homer and Plato stand and fall together in this particular context. If we must reject Homer's wisdom, because the form of the Homeric poems is unsuitable to the young of the ideal republic, we must do exactly the same with Plato's dialogues, and for the same reasons.

[32] Compare 195.13-18.

"What does this (i.e. Plato's proscription) have to do with Homer's poetry? It adequately describes tragedy and comedy. For these are representations wholly fashioned with the audience's entertainment in mind. But it is not at all appropriate to Homer's poems, since they have their source in the Gods and reveal to us the nature of reality. For how can that poetic form be termed 'mimetic' which interprets for us, through the medium of symbols, the divine realm? For symbols are not representations of those things of which they are symbols, since that which is the contrary of something else cannot be a representation of that thing, such as the ugly of the beautiful or that which is contrary to nature or that which is natural. For symbolic wisdom (*theoria*) hints at the nature of reality through the medium of elements totally contrary in their nature. Therefore, if a poet is inspired and reveals the truth through symbols (*synthemata*), or if one making use of philosophical knowledge reveals to us the very structure of reality, this man is neither a mimetic artist nor can he (i.e. his art) be refuted by the previous arguments."
(I. 198.8-24)

Proclus considers a new point (202.9-205.24) related to what has preceded, but in a strict sense distinct. That is the claim made for Homer that he is an educator of men.[33] But if Homer was an educator of his fellow citizens, why does Plato say that he is not? "For he (i.e. Plato) was surely not unaware of the arguments we have rehearsed nor of what he had written elsewhere" (202.11-12). Proclus' answer, on the whole, rests on the biographical consideration that Plato's position is, in some way, explicable by the insufficient esteem in which philosophy was held by his contemporaries, who "admired poetry beyond all measure and supposed that it alone sufficed for education." [34] It was the same "good intentions" which prompted him to attack the sophists as well. But his attacks were chiefly aimed, according to Proclus, at the "tragedians" and all those imitative artists who "contrived the means of bewitch-

---

[33] In support of this Proclus offers two lines of argument, the first historical, the second a rather jumbled rehearsal of previous points. The historical argument is as follows. We know that certain cities, after Homer's death, used his poems to settle disputes. We also know that wise men like Pythagoras, Lycurgus and Solon were turned to by their contemporaries for advice and instruction in political matters. Therefore, we must conclude that the same was true of Homer, and that the reason we have no historical record of it is that the "length of time has destroyed the memory of these events which had been (before then) handed down by men." (200.9-11).

[34] This is curiously like the main argument of Eric Havelock in his *Preface to Plato* (Cambridge, U.S.A., 1963).

ing the minds of the audience, but who had created no way of helping them towards moral excellence." And it was because Homer was the "founder (*archegon*) of this kind of poetry and had provided the tragedians with the seeds of their imitative art, that Plato judged him worthy of similar rebukes." For this reason Plato "relaxed his reverential attitude toward Homer and, ranking him with the tragedians as an imitative artist, censured him." But it is only in this circumscribed way that we must understand Homer's banishment. "For as far as his knowledge is concerned, he has the same understanding of reality as Plato, but, as one who has something in common with the tragic poets, he is exiled from the well-governed state." [35]

I have suggested that Plato's attitude toward poetry, complex and ambiguous as it was, greatly facilitated the task of even the most loyal and reverential Platonist who felt moved to write a defence of poetry. In this matter certain points should be kept in mind. First, Plato nowhere states that allegorical "undersenses" do not exist; he merely argues that the possible fact of their existence in a specific text is of no relevance to the educational problems examined in Books II-III of the *Republic*. Secondly, it seems clear that Plato *genuinely* believed that the poets were, in fact, often inspired; if there is any irony in his attitude, it is directed toward their claims that such truth as their poetry contains can be thought of as knowledge or be of any primary importance to philosophers. Thirdly, as we have already argued, Plato clearly is sympathetic to poetry and to other art forms, provided, of course, that they rest on philosophical bases; he is thus in no sense, *in principle*, opposed to art. Lastly, in the tenth book of the *Republic*, Socrates rejects poetry only in so far as it is *imitation*, and what imitation means, in this context, does seem to be indicated by the example of the Bed, where the imitative nature of art is defined as the simple copying of external, phenomenal reality. It is no cause for wonder that the Neoplatonists assumed that Plato believed there were other kinds of poetry.

In view of these facts, it is not surprising that Proclus should have been able to "rescue" Homer. Exploiting Plato's remarks about the "divine" and "inspired" Homer, as well as his failure explicitly to deny the existence of allegorical meanings, Proclus

---

[35] Compare 204.7-8.

read back into Homer's text the metaphysical universe of late Neoplatonism and, in the process, endowed with an abundant reality that ill-defined and only negatively implied species of poetry which for Plato belonged to the category of the non-mimetic.

4. POETIC MATTER AND STYLE IN NEOPLATONIC THEORY

So much, then, for the poet and the art of poetry. We have seen that the activity of the writer was primarily thought of in terms of purpose or intention. This purpose, also conceived of as the end or the good of the dialogue, constituted the microcosmic analogue of the Godhead of the Universe. But there were other correspondences, and we must now consider the question of what elements in a work of literature corresponded to macrocosmic form and matter.

> "In the dialogue what corresponds to matter are the characters, and the time and place in which Plato set his dialogues."
> (*Anon. Proleg.* 16.7-8, tr. Westerink)

And just as in the Macrocosm matter is subject to Divine purpose, so, too, in Plato's dialogues the "matter" can never constitute, by itself, the purpose of the dialogue, but is, of necessity, always subordinate to this purpose:

> "There still remains the necessity of looking for the chief purpose of the dialogue and of considering how all of these elements (which have been previously discussed) fit whatever the purpose of the dialogue is shown to be by our discussion. For all that we have said up to now we have said with reference to the prologues of the dialogue and to the arguments concerning the forms. . . . Just as there is a path of ascent from the phenomenal world to the intelligible, so, too, we must return from the circumstantial details which make up the subject of the dialogue to that single purpose and one goal of the whole composition, and we must subordinate to this, as best we can, all that we have previously considered in isolation, i.e. the characters, the time, and the place."
> (Proclus, *In Parmenidem*, 630.21-36)

The consequence of this view is, of course, that the mise-en-scène, every narrative detail, every aspect of a character—his birth-place, physical gestures, remarks, even his name—will be viewed as directly expressive of their creator's purpose and as demanding immediate interpretive participation on the part of the reader.

Thus Plato, in the *Parmenides* (126B) has the Clazomenian visitor say, in his effort to obtain an interview with Antiphon,

"These men, I said, are my fellow-citizens, and most interested in philosophy. They have heard that this Antiphon has often met with a certain Pythodorus, who was a friend of Zeno, and that through often having heard Pythodorus, he (Antiphon) remembers the discussion which Socrates, Zeno, and Parmenides once held."

With regard to this passage, two things seemed worthy of note to Proclus. First, the exact route by which the original discussion was transmitted; secondly the addition of qualifiers ('this' and 'a certain') before the names of Antiphon and Pythodorus, when none had been placed before the names of Socrates, Zeno, and Parmenides. In Proclus' view, this series of removes represented a thinning out or multiplication of reality from a unified source. Antiphon and Pythodorus, he says, are "images of more specific or particular levels of reality" (*Par.* 673.10-14), and it is thus appropriate that qualifying or limiting words, such as "this" or "a certain," should be attached to their names. This is familiar exegesis, and can be paralleled in many passages. What is of more than casual interest, however, is the explicit formulation of the degree of intention involved in Plato's allegorical uses of these characters.

> "*Consider also how he* (*i.e. Plato*) *looks up again at his models* (*i.e. the intelligible world*) *and says* that Pythorodus 'often' met Zeno and Antiphon 'often' met Pythodorus."
> (672.37-673.4) [36]

Or,

> "See, again, how he has assigned the appropriate level (of reality) to his characters."
> (672.14-15)

And because this is so, the reader, in a reverse movement—that is, from copy to model—will be able to say with Proclus,

> "It is obvious from what has been said how one is to relate these details to intelligible reality."
> (672.20-22)

Not only in the characters themselves, however, but also the location in which the action of the dialogue unfolds and, rather curiously, even the *time* when it occurs were thought of as material elements subordinate to the aim of the dialogue. Although there

---

[36] Proclus (673.4-8) explains the word 'often' in this passage as symbolic of the increased multiplicity of those states of being with which, in his view, Pythodorus and Antiphon are to be associated (see 628.39-629.20).

will be some disagreement among modern critics concerning the degree of consciousness involved on Plato's part, there is no question that the assumptions we are outlining can lead the interpreter to the formulation of extremely fruitful questions. One may not readily agree with Proclus' explanation of Plato's reasons for setting the *Republic* in the Peiraeus on the occasion of the festival of Bendis. However, when Hermeias says (*In Phaedrum* 18.20-23) that it is "quite consistent that the licentious Lysias should be represented as staying at the house of the glutton Morychus," a modern reader will likely find this a judicious observation.[37]

Characters, time and place. The Neoplatonic commentators also devoted their attention at times to more comprehensive literary structures. We have already had occasion to discuss the passage in which the "chain of transmission" [38] described in the *Parmenides* was taken as a microcosmic analogue of the interconnected levels of reality. Such reports are, as the *Anon. Proleg.* (20.9-12) observes, never at more than a third remove from the original discussion. Accordingly, the author notes, "In this matter, also, it is clear that Plato is representing the structure of reality. For this structure does not go beyond three removes, since all things are either perceived by intellect, etc."

Characters with certain attributes can thus converse at a certain time, in a certain place and in explicit structural relationships to one another. But since Platonic dialogue is also a narrative of what these characters say and do, their words and actions, too, were regularly thought of by the exegetes as direct expressions of Plato's intention rather than as, in the manner of the rhetorical critics, an image of the speaker's character. As Hermeias puts the matter with regard to actions (*In Phaedrum* 33.3-4), "Gestures, too, must be portrayed in a way which accords with the theme of the dialogue." [39]

---

[37] For a Platonist, of course, time (as opposed to eternity) is an aspect of the material world (cf. *Timaeus* 37C-38D). For a discussion of these points, see *Anonymous Prolegomena* 16.8-18, 35-41 and 42-48 with parallels cited. 'Festival of Bendis': see Proclus, *In Rempublicam*, 1, ed. Kroll, 17.1-18.7 and 18.7-19.23. 'Judicious observation': I happen to believe that Morychus' gluttony is thematically significant, but even if one disputes this point the fact remains that certain varieties of literary interpretation are precluded if one does not assign any real value to this kind of detail.

[38] 'Chain of transmission': literally, 'manner of association' (*tropos tes synousias*). The phrase is used in a somewhat different sense at 17.16-24.

[39] Compare also, in the same commentary, 25.24-27 and 27.4-10.

The question of speech, however, is a bit more complicated. For convenience of discussion, and with acknowledgement of the blurrings involved, I should like to propose that we consider the question of speech (as opposed to action and other narrative elements) under three headings: argument (i.e. philosophical proof), diction (i.e. the choice of discrete lexical units, without reference to their "total effect"), and, lastly, style (i.e. just such a "total effect"). The first two elements can be treated rather briefly. Philosophical proofs, in the schema of the *Anonymous Prolegomena* to which we have often referred, correspond to "soul" in the macrocosm.[40] On the other hand, diction as such, i.e. individual words *qua* words, is not explicitly related to any macrocosmic element. But, if we may take a lead from several of Proclus' remarks in his *Cratylus* commentary, it appears that words, as such, are conceived of as *material* or phenomenal images of intelligible reality, and are thus very similar to gestures and actions, which are also material manifestations of a character's as well as of the author's intent.[41]

This is, doubtless, the Neoplatonists' way of stating the obvious, that is, that words express thoughts, but the special character this gives to verbal exegesis is nonetheless significant. If in the rhetorical tradition the choice of words is viewed primarily from the point of view of their function in expressing character (i.e. "This is the *kind* of word a man like that would use."), in the Neoplatonic commentaries the question usually asked is, "How does the choice of this particular word, or group of words, reflect the *intention* of the author?" Thus, in reference to the opening words of the *Ist Alcibiades* ("O son of Cleinias, I suppose you are *wondering* why it is that although I was the first of your lovers I still continue when all others have stopped"), Proclus will remark that Plato, "in the very first words of the dialogue is showing us in an excellent way the whole theme of his work" (19.9-10). Considerable exegesis follows, but at length (42.5-43.1) Proclus observes that in attributing "wonder" to Alcibiades, Plato is making clear to us, wonder being the beginning of philosophy (cf. *Theaetetus*

---

[40] See above, note 13.

[41] See Proclus *in Cratylum*, ed. Pasquali (Leipzig, 1908). Words have form *and* matter (4.16-18, cf. 8.11-13); words are 'images' (*eikones*) of transcendent reality (3.10-11, cf. 6.11-14, 11.2-4). Of course, even the *letters* of a word can be thought of as material images of an unseen world; see, F. Dornseiff, *Das Alphabet in Mystik und Magie* [2] (Leipzig, 1925), esp. pp. 1-2.

155D), that Alcibiades is in a state of readiness for that initial investigation into the nature of the Self which is the subject of the *Alcibiades*.[42]

The broader question of style, that is, the way we are made to perceive something said or done—its aura or texture—is also treated. Let us recall our schema from the *Anonymous Prolegomena*. If the characters, setting, etc., are the *material* elements, i.e. the subject matter, then literary style (17.1-15, *charakter*) finds its analogues in enveloping *form*, that by which matter is given shape and definition. This correspondence we find explicitly in the chronologically earlier commentaries of Proclus.[43] Indeed, as we already saw, it goes back in some form to at least the fourth century B.C., without however being a part of anything remotely like the developed Neoplatonic context we are now studying.

Here, too, if we make a comparison with the rhetorical critics, we discern both similarity and contrast. Both groups of critics will determine the success of a given style in terms of its *appropriateness*. But appropriateness is rather differently defined in either case. For the rhetorical critics—and we are no doubt simplifying somewhat—a certain style was felt to be appropriate if it suited the character of a particular person (whether he himself spoke or was described) or of a particular event. The Neoplatonists, however, conceived of the matter somewhat differently, and although there is probably less of a real difference in this matter than in anything we have hitherto examined, we should nonetheless try to perceive that difference. What this was can be illustrated by a passage from Proclus. He is discussing the simile which Plato uses in *Timaeus* (19B).

> "I feel rather like a man who has been looking at some noble creatures in a painting, or perhaps at real animals, alive but motionless, and conceives a desire to watch them in motion and actively exercising the powers promised by their form."
> (tr. Cornford)

After rehearsing the views of other commentators about the relevance of Socrates' remarks to the task of describing the ideal republic in operation, Proclus states his own position:

---

[42] For this reason, the dialogue was the first to be read in the Neoplatonic curriculum, cf. *Anonymous Prolegomena*, 26.18-20.

[43] Westerink, in his note on this passage, cites the parallels.

"We should be inclined to say that this comparison was also employed by Plato because the ideal republic (i.e. in Socrates' resumé) was portrayed in the likeness of divine things, and the charm of the diction conveys an image of the charm with which the heavenly realm has been endowed by the Demiurge. We should further say that the blending of an artificial element, style, with what is natural conveys an image of divine creativity (*poiesis*), because this, too, has both a self-derived limit (like art) and, as well, something which (continually) proceeds from being and essence (like nature)."
(*In Timaeum*, I.60.4-11)

Now it may plausibly be argued that only a critic with distinctly Platonist leanings would be likely to speak of style in such a way. It does seem remote from the thinking of the rhetorical critics to argue that the quality of Plato's style in the passage, i.e. the mixture of the artificial and natural, is an intentional rendering of some fundamental attribute of the universe. Nonetheless, there probably is little real difference, apart from the manner of describing the process of stylistic mimesis, between Neoplatonic and rhetorical formulations. In both cases, it would seem, style is thought of as imitation, and, although the object of imitation differs in either case, in both views style seeks to reproduce some characteristic of that object.

Indeed, and on this point we conclude our discussion of style, the subject itself seems to be one for which the Neoplatonists entertained, at best, ambivalent feelings. They were eager, on the one hand, to underscore the functional and non-ornamental character of Plato's style. For their master never calculated simply to charm the ear of the listener; his style was, as we saw, the image of a higher, intelligible reality. On the other hand, style, although it possessed importance from this particular standpoint, was in the larger view, of distinctly secondary value. What is of importance is not style itself, but the intelligible realm of which it is a reflection. In discussing *Timaeus* 21A, "I shall tell you an old tale I heard from a man who was not young," Proclus, after outlining the views of Longinus, Origen, and Arostoxenus on the stylistic qualities of the sentence, concludes in a rather petulant way:

"The great Iamblichus prefers that we refer the stylistic variety to higher realities, and that we see how, in nature too, opposites are contained in the One and how the One becomes various and how

great is the variety which the same principles of reality (*logoi*)
exhibit, for they are one way when they are present in the Mind of
the Cosmos, another when in the Soul, another when in Nature,
another when, at the lowest level, having become matter, they
exhibit very great heterogeneity along with similarity. These are
the matters which are worthy of the thought of Plato, not some
fussy attention to diction."
(Proclus, *In Timaeum*, 87.6-15)

CONCLUSION

The final significance of the Neoplatonists' contribution to literary theory lies in the fact that they restored to the interpretation of texts a philosophical breadth and rigor which had all but vanished in the centuries which intervened between their own time and the era of Plato and Aristotle. One may argue that in the Judeo-Christian interpretative tradition figures like Philo, Clement of Alexandria, Origen and Saint Augustine were not without theoretical power and originality. But this objection is, in the end, irrelevant because it fails to take into account the fact that in literary theory, as in so many other areas of thought, paganism was very little affected by Jewish and Christian speculation. A modern scholar is able to look back upon the first five Christian centuries and impose a kind of intellectual unity upon the varied whole. Yet it remains true that within that whole, for reasons which more often than not reflected intellectual arrogance on the part of the pagans, the Greco-Roman tradition of literary thought continued to be a fairly self-contained universe. And in that universe not even the most notable figures of the post-Aristotelian period, Cicero, Quintilian, "Longinus," exhibited anything like the theoretical power of the Neoplatonists. To be sure, if we were by some fortunate chance to recover lost works of commentators of the Hellenistic period, in particular the Stoic commentators on Homer, this assertion might well need revision, but it seems true in the light of our present knowledge.

The matters to which the Neoplatonists turned their speculative energies must be ranked among the most difficult and unyielding problems of literary theory. What, for example, is the exact nature of the relationship between a work of literary representation and the object, or objects, of representation? Is it possible for a single detail in a literary text to have, not one, but multiple, even numberless referents? Again, what is the relationship between the structure of a literary text and the structure of reality as a whole? If one allows some such relationship, can one go so far as to postulate a thoroughgoing macrocosmic-microcosmic analogy? Moreover, if we think of a literary artifact as somehow analogous to a living organism, how are we to understand and identify what, in a literary work, corresponds to the kind of unity which is characteristic of biological organisms? How, last of all, does the assumption of conscious intention on the part of the author affect the critical procedures of the interpreter?

These are all basic questions. In the process of attempting their solution the Neoplatonists committed themselves in a fundamental way to the assumption that the special reality of a literary text was the precise analogue, in all significant respects, of the larger reality of the world as a whole, this larger reality being, of course, systematically understood along Neoplatonist lines. The result was that literary texts, for their part, came to be thought of as microcosms endowed with a specifically Neoplatonic metaphysical structure.

This assumption, whatever its ultimate merit or validity, engendered a number of fruitful and stimulating theoretical conclusions. By transferring to literary texts basic assumptions and methods of analysis which characterized Neoplatonic thought in general, the commentators were able to formulate impressive solutions to the questions just enunciated. To take one example. Unity is, as is well known, a most important concept in Neoplatonic thought. For the Neoplatonists the source of both the being and the intelligibility of the universe was that primal, undifferentiated unity out of which every aspect of perceived reality proceeded and to which it in turn reverted. Without this Oneness the world could neither be nor be understood, being and intelligibility, in the view of the Neoplatonists, necessarily implying each other. By conceiving of a literary text according to such a model, answers to certain questions suggested themselves. If in the world at large every element partakes to some degree of Oneness, so, too, in the literary microcosm, every element, however seemingly trivial, is significant because it arises from the unified source of the work's being, that is, the author's controlling intellect, and must be interpreted accordingly. Again, for the Neoplatonists the status of all the varied forms of differentiated reality generated from the One were by no means equal. The universe of the later Neoplatonists is a relentlessly hierarchical structure. The consequence is that every differentiated element within it, save for the highest and the lowest, in addition to being derivative of the One, also enjoys a secondary relationship of relative superiority or inferiority to other 'cognate' elements according as these partake more or less of Oneness. The Neoplatonic universe is thus a vast cosmic order marked by the greatest rigidity, and within that order everything "knows its place." This more complex metaphysical structure, by becoming a model for literary artifacts, facilitated other kinds of solutions. If, in an analysis of Being, one could begin at the lowest levels of reality and proceed step-wise to the One through a series of stages, each distinct and each progressively more and more imbued with unity, then one could also argue that elements which make up the surface of the text were only the lowest manifestations of a virtually endless series of distinct *stages*—in an exegetical context, *meanings*—which had their ultimate source in the intellect of the author, in this view, the unified source of the work's meanings. It would seem, at least, that this latter was the operating assumption. It may have been, however, that the Neoplatonists felt justified in reading Homer "symbolically," simply because they believed that Homer, in his inspired wisdom, had created a true image of the world and that his poems must therefore be read with exactly the same presuppositions as the world itself was "read." In fact, it should be clear that, given Neoplatonic premises with regard to the authors they revered, Homer, Hesiod, Plato and "Orpheus," unity was never really called into doubt, since it was a theoretically necessary aspect of every such text. Unity was a given, in certain kinds of literature as in reality; it was the exegete's task to discover how, in each particular case, this general truth was to be demonstrated.

It should also be pointed out that literary organicism, which before the Neoplatonists was limited to what seem exclusively biological analogues, now gained a literally cosmic context. Because the Macrocosm of the Neoplatonists, in accordance with Plato's views, was conceived as a great Living Thing, the analogous literary microcosm, too, became in this specifically new and wider sense "organic."

As a corollary to the assumption that a work of literature was the microcosmic analogue of the Great Cosmos, a noteworthy innovation was introduced into the centuries long tradition of the glorification of Homer and the other early poets of Greece. One feature in this tradition was that the epithet "divine" or "god-like" was applied to Homer with the greatest frequency. What the epithet meant, of course, was that Homer was considered a divinely inspired spokesman of knowledge which, under ordinary circumstances, would have remained unrevealed to mortals, the possession of the

APPENDIX

GREEK TEXTS OF THE NEOPLATONIC COMMENTATORS

The passages which follow are from the editions cited in the Bibliography. The commentaries are listed according to usual procedures: author and work are listed alphabetically, and then, under each work, passages are given in the sequence in which they occur in that work, and not in the order in which they are discussed in the body of the book. The original of any translated passage, however, ought to be found without difficulty.

Anonymous Prolegomena 15.1-7

Δεῖ οὖν εἰπεῖν τὰς αἰτίας δι᾽ ἃς τοιούτῳ εἴδει συγγραφῆς ἐχρήσατο. λέγομεν τοίνυν ὅτι τοῦτο ἐποίησεν ἐπειδὴ ὁ διάλογος οἷον κόσμος ἐστίν. ὥσπερ γὰρ ἐν τῷ διαλόγῳ διάφορα πρόσωπά εἰσιν φθεγγόμενα καθὼς ἑκάστῳ πρέπει, οὕτω καὶ ἐν τῷ ὅλῳ κόσμῳ διάφοροί εἰσιν φύσεις φθογγὴν διάφορον ἀφιεῖσαι· φθέγγεται γὰρ ἕκαστος κατὰ τὴν οἰκείαν φύσιν. μιμούμενος οὖν τὰ θεῖα δημιουργήματα, τὸν κόσμον λέγω, καὶ τοῦτο ἐποίησεν.

ibid. 16.1-8

Πέμπτον ἐπὶ τοῖς εἰρημένοις κεφάλαιον ζητήσωμεν πόσα ἐστὶν τὰ συνιστῶντα ἕκαστον τῶν Πλάτωνος διαλόγων. ἐπεὶ τοίνυν μεμαθήκαμεν ὡς ὁ διάλογος κόσμος ἐστὶν καὶ ὁ κόσμος διάλογος, ὅσα εἰσὶν τὰ συνιστῶντα τὸν κόσμον, τοσαῦτα καὶ τοὺς διαλόγους εὑρήσομεν. εἰσὶν τοίνυν ἐν τῷ ὅλῳ κόσμῳ ὕλη, εἶδος, φύσις ἡ τὸ εἶδος ἐνθεῖσα τῇ ὕλῃ, ψυχή, νοῦς, καὶ θεότης.

᾿Εν δὲ τῷ διαλόγῳ ἀναλογεῖ μὲν τῇ ὕλῃ τὰ πρόσωπα καὶ ὁ χρόνος καὶ ὁ τόπος ἐν ᾧ τοὺς διαλόγους ἔγραψεν ὁ Πλάτων.

ibid. 21.2-7

῎Εννατον ἐπὶ τοῖς εἰρημένοις δεῖ ζητῆσαι κεφάλαιον, ἐκ πόσων κανόνων δεῖ θηρᾶν τὸν ἑκάστου διαλόγου σκοπόν. χρεία γάρ ἐστιν τοῦτον ζητεῖν, ἐπειδὴ ὡς αὐτὸς λέγει ἐν Φαίδρῳ ῾ὦ παῖ, μία τίς ἐστιν ὁδὸς τοῖς μέλλουσι καλῶς βουλεύεσθαι, εἰδέναι περὶ οὗ ἂν ᾖ ἡ βουλή· ἐπειδὴ τοῦ παντὸς ἁμαρτάνειν ἀνάγκη᾽. πῶς οὖν αὐτοῦ τοῦτο λέγοντος παραιτησόμεθα ἐπὶ τῶν αὐτοῦ συγγραμμάτων τὸ εἰδέναι περὶ τίνος ἐν ἑκάστῳ διαλέγεται;

9*

Hermeias, *In Phaedrum* 231.6-9

Διὰ τί δὲ ἡνωμένον δεῖ τὸν λόγον εἶναι; ἐπειδὴ παντὶ πράγματι τὸ καλὸν καὶ τὸ εὖ ἀπὸ τοῦ ἑνὸς ἐπιλάμπεται· εἰ μὴ γὰρ τῷ ἑνὶ κατασχεθῇ, οἷον δήποτε πρᾶγμα οὐ δύναται εἶναι ἀγαθόν· οὕτως καὶ τὸ κάλλος οὐκ ἔστι καλὸν εἰ μὴ ἕνωσις γένηται πάντων τῶν μορίων.

Olympiodorus, *In Alcibiadem* 56.14-18

ἤ, ὥς φησιν ἐν τῷ Φαίδρῳ, 'δεῖ τὸν λόγον ἐοικέναι ζῴῳ'· καὶ τὸν οὖν ἄριστα κατεσκευασμένον λόγον δεῖ τῷ ἀρίστῳ τῶν ζῴων ἐοικέναι. ἄριστον δὲ ζῷον ὁ κόσμος· ὥσπερ οὖν οὗτος λειμών ἐστι ποικίλων ζῴων, οὕτω δεῖ καὶ τὸν λόγον εἶναι πλήρη παντοδαπῶν προσώπων.

Proclus, *Elements of Theology*, Prop. 140

140. Πᾶσαι τῶν θεῶν αἱ δυνάμεις ἄνωθεν ἀρχόμεναι καὶ διὰ τῶν οἰκείων προϊοῦσαι μεσοτήτων μέχρι τῶν ἐσχάτων καθήκουσι καὶ τῶν περὶ γῆν τόπων.

οὔτε γὰρ ἐκείνας διείργει τι καὶ ἀποκωλύει τῆς εἰς πάντα παρουσίας (οὐδὲ γὰρ δέονται τόπων καὶ διαστάσεων, διὰ τὴν ἄσχετον πρὸς πάντα ὑπεροχὴν καὶ τὴν ἄμικτον πανταχοῦ παρουσίαν), οὔτε τὸ μετέχειν αὐτῶν ἐπιτήδειον κωλύεται τῆς μεθέξεως, ἀλλ᾽ ἅμα τέ τι πρὸς τὴν μετουσίαν ἕτοιμον γίνεται κἀκεῖναι πάρεισιν, οὔτε τότε παραγενόμεναι οὔτε πρότερον ἀποῦσαι, ἀλλ᾽ ἀεὶ ὡσαύτως ἔχουσαι. ἐὰν οὖν τι τῶν περὶ γῆν ἐπιτήδειον ᾖ μετέχειν, καὶ τούτῳ πάρεισι· καὶ πάντα πεπληρώκασιν ἑαυτῶν, καὶ τοῖς μὲν ὑπερτέροις μειζόνως πάρεισι, τοῖς δὲ μέσοις κατὰ τὴν αὐτῶν τάξιν, τοῖς δὲ ἐσχάτοις ἐσχάτως. ἄνωθεν οὖν μέχρι τῶν τελευταίων ἐκτείνουσιν ἑαυτάς· ὅθεν καὶ ἐν τούτοις εἰσὶ τῶν πρώτων ἐμφάσεις, καὶ συμπαθῆ πάντα πᾶσιν, ἐν μὲν τοῖς πρώτοις τῶν δευτέρων προϋπαρχόντων, ἐν δὲ τοῖς δευτέροις τῶν πρώτων ἐμφαινομένων· τριχῶς γὰρ ἦν ἕκαστον, ἢ κατ᾽ αἰτίαν ἢ καθ᾽ ὕπαρξιν ἢ κατὰ μέθεξιν.

Proclus, *In Alcibiadem* 18.13-19.10

Τὰ προοίμια τῶν Πλατωνικῶν διαλόγων συνᾴδει πρὸς τοὺς ὅλους αὐτῶν σκοπούς, καὶ οὔτε δραματικῆς ἕνεκα ψυχαγωγίας μεμηχάνηται τῷ Πλάτωνι (πόρρω γάρ ἐστιν ὁ τρόπος οὗτος τῆς συγγραφῆς τῆς τοῦ φιλοσόφου μεγαλοφροσύνης) οὔτε τῆς ἱστορίας στοχάζεται μόνης, ὥσπερ τινὲς ὑπειλήφασιν· οὔτε γὰρ πιθανόν ἐστιν οὔθ᾽ ὅλως δυνατόν, ἅπαντα ἐξῆς ἀπὸ τῶν γεγονότων ἢ ῥηθέντων λαμβάνεσθαι πρὸς τὴν μίαν τῶν Πλατωνικῶν συγγραμμάτων τελείωσιν· ἀλλ᾽ ὥσπερ καὶ τοῖς ἡμετέροις δοκεῖ καθηγεμόσι καὶ ἡμῖν ἐν ἄλλοις μετρίως ὑπέμνησται, τῆς ὅλης τῶν διαλόγων ἐξήρτηται καὶ ταῦτα προθέσεως, καὶ τὰ μὲν ἐκ τῶν ὑποκειμένων πραγμάτων ἢ λόγων συναρμόζεται πρὸς τὸν παρόντα σκοπόν, τὰ δὲ τελειοῦται τῶν ἐλλειπόντων εἰς τὴν τῆς προκειμένης θεωρίας συμπλήρωσιν, ὁμοῦ δὲ πάντα καθάπερ ἐν τελετῇ πρὸς τὴν ὅλην ἀνάγεται τῶν ζητουμένων τελείωσιν. τοῦτο δὴ οὖν μοι δοκεῖ καὶ ἐν τούτῳ τῷ διαλόγῳ προτείνειν ἡμῖν ὁ Πλάτων τὸ δόγμα, καὶ καλῶς ἐπιδεικνύναι δι' αὐτῆς τῆς πρωτίστης ἐπιβολῆς τῶν λόγων τὸν σύμπαντα τοῦ γράμματος σκοπόν.

Proclus, *In Parmenidem* 630.21-36

Τούτων δὲ ἡμῖν προδιατεταγμένων, ἀναγκαία λοιπόν ἐστιν ἡ τοῦ σκοποῦ ζήτησις καὶ ἡ θεωρία, πῶς ἅπαντα ταῦτα πρὸς τὸν ἕνα συνήρτηται τοῦ διαλόγου σκοπόν, ὃν ἂν φήνῃ ὁ λόγος· ὅσα γὰρ προείπομεν, εἰς τὰ προοίμια τοῦ διαλόγου βλέποντες εἴπομεν, καὶ τοὺς περὶ τῶν ἰδεῶν λόγους, ἀφ' ὧν καὶ ἐπιγράφειν αὐτόν τινες, ὡς εἴρηται, τῶν ἔμπροσθεν ἠξίωσαν. Δεῖ γάρ, ὥσπερ ἐκ τῶν φαινομένων ἐπὶ τὸ νοητὸν ἡ ἄνοδος, οὕτω καὶ ἡμᾶς ἀπὸ τῶν ὑποκειμένων τῷ διαλόγῳ περιστατικῶν ἐπὶ τὴν μίαν ἀναδραμεῖν τῶν λόγων πρόθεσιν καὶ τὸ ἓν τέλος τῆς ὅλης πραγματείας ταύτης, τούτῳ δὲ καὶ τὰ ἄλλα συντάττειν εἰς δύναμιν τὰ πρόσωπα, τοὺς καιρούς, τοὺς τόπους, πάντα ὅσα πρότερον αὐτὰ καθ' αὑτὰ τεθεωρήκαμεν.

ibid. 658.33-659.23

'Αλλὰ περὶ μὲν τούτου πλείω τῶν ἀναγκαίων εἴπομεν. 'Επανιτέον δὲ εἰς τὰ προκείμενα, καὶ τοσοῦτον προσθετέον ὅτι τῶν παλαιῶν περὶ τῶν Πλατωνικῶν προοιμίων διαφόρους δόξας ἐχόντων, καὶ τῶν μὲν εἰς τὴν τούτων ἐξέτασιν οὐδ' ὅλως καθιέντων (ἥκειν γὰρ χρῆναι ταῦτα προακηκοότας τοὺς τῶν δογμάτων ἐραστὰς γνησίους), τῶν δὲ οὐδὲ τούτων ὡς ἔτυχεν ἀκροωμένων, ἀλλὰ τὴν χρείαν αὐτῶν εἰς καθηκόντων ὑπογραφὰς ἀναπεμπόντων καὶ τὴν πρὸς τὰ ζητούμενα ἐν τοῖς διαλόγοις οἰκονομίαν διδασκόντων, τῶν δὲ καὶ ταῦτα πρὸς τὴν τῶν πραγμάτων φύσιν ἀξιούντων τοὺς ἐξηγητὰς ἀνάγειν, ἑπόμενοι καὶ ἡμεῖς τούτοις προηγουμένην ποιησόμεθα τὴν πρὸς τὰ πράγματα τοῦ προοιμίου τὰ προκείμενα φέρουσαν ἀνάπτυξιν. Οὐ μὴν οὐδὲ τῆς τῶν καθηκόντων ἀμελήσομεν ἐπιστάσεως. Δεῖ γὰρ ἐπὶ τῶν Πλάτωνος διαλόγων εἰς τὰ πράγματα βλέπειν διαφερόντως τὰ ὑποκείμενα τῷ διαλόγῳ, καὶ σκοπεῖν ὅπως καὶ τὰ προοίμια ταῦτα ἐνεικονίζεται, καὶ ἓν ἀποφαίνειν ζῶον ἐκ πάντων τῶν μερῶν ἑαυτῷ συμφωνοῦν, ἕκαστον ἀπειργασμένον, ὡς αὐτὸς ἐν Φαίδρῳ φησί, καὶ τούτοις συναρμόττειν, καὶ ὅσα τοῦ τύπου τούτου τῶν καθηκόντων ἐστί· τὸ δὲ παντελῶς ἀλλότρια τὰ προοίμια τῶν ἑπομένων εἶναι, καθάπερ τὰ τῶν 'Ηρακλείδου τοῦ Ποντικοῦ καὶ Θεοφράστου διαλόγων, πᾶσαν ἀνίᾳ κρίσεως μετέχουσαν ἀκοήν.

ibid. 672.14-22

Καὶ ὅρα πάλιν ὅπως τοῖς προσώποις αὐτὸς τὴν πρέπουσαν τάξιν ἀποδέδωκε· τὸν μὲν γὰρ Ἀντιφῶντα ὑποτάττει τῷ Πυθοδώρῳ, τοῦτον δὲ τῷ Ζήνωνι· καὶ πάλιν τῆς πρὸ τούτων τριάδος, τὸν μὲν Σωκράτη τίθησιν ὡς ἐγγυτέρω τῶν περὶ τὸν Κέφαλον, δεύτερον δὲ τὸν Ζήνωνα, τρίτον δὲ τὸν Παρμενίδην· ὅπως δὲ ταῦτα ἐπὶ τὰ πράγματα ἀνενεκτέον, οὐκ ἄδηλον ἐκ τῶν εἰρημένων.

ibid. 672.37-673.4

ὅρα δὲ ὅπως πάλιν εἰς τὰ παραδείγματα ἀποβλέπων καὶ τὸν Πυθόδωρον πολλάκις ἐντετυχηκέναι τῷ Ζήνωνί φησι, καὶ τὸν Ἀντιφῶντα τοῦ Πυθοδώρου πολλάκις ἀκηκοέναι·

Proclus, *In Rempublicam*, vol. I. 11.7-13

· · · ἀλλ' εἶναι περί τε πολιτείας τὴν πρόθεσιν καὶ τῆς ὡς ἀληθῶς δικαιοσύνης, οὐχ ὡς δύο τῶν σκοπῶν ὄντων (οὐδὲ γὰρ δυνατόν· δεῖ γοῦν ἐπείπερ ζῴῳ προσέοικεν ὁ λόγος, οὗ τι καὶ ὄφελός ἐστιν, ἕνα σκοπὸν ἔχειν, ὥσπερ πᾶν ζῷον πρὸς τὰ μέρη πάντα συντέτακται κατὰ | μίαν ὁμολογίαν), ἀλλ' ὡς τῶν δύο τούτων ἀλλήλοις τῶν αὐτῶν ὄντων.

ibid. 69.23-70.21

Ἔναγχος ἡμῖν ἐν τοῖς τοῦ Πλάτωνος γενεθλίοις διαλεγομένοις παρέστη διασκέψασθαι, τίνα ἄν τις τρόπον ὑπέρ τε Ὁμήρου πρὸς τὸν ἐν Πολιτείᾳ Σωκράτη τοὺς προσήκοντας ποιήσαιτο λόγους καὶ ἐπιδείξειεν τῇ τε φύσει τῶν πραγμάτων καὶ τοῖς αὐτῷ ‹τῷ› φιλοσόφῳ μάλιστα πάντων ἀρέσκουσιν συμφωνότατα περί τε τῶν θείων καὶ τῶν ἀνθρωπίνων ἀναδιδάσκοντα, καὶ τὸν Πλάτωνα τῆς πρὸς ἑαυτὸν ἐξέλοι διαφωνίας, καὶ ἀποφήνειεν ὡς ἄρα ἐκ μιᾶς ἐπιστήμης ἅπαντα καὶ νοερᾶς ἐπιβλέψεως καὶ προαιρέσεως θεοπρεποῦς, ὅσα τε ἐγκωμιάζων γέγραφεν τὴν Ὁμήρου ποίησιν καὶ ὅσα | ἐπαιτιώμενος ἔφθεγκται. καὶ γὰρ ἄν τις ἀπορήσειεν εἰς ταῦτα ἀποβλέψας, εἰ μὲν ὀρθῶς ὁ Πλάτων αὐτὸν ἐλέγχειν προὔθετο καὶ δεικνύναι τῆς προσηκούσης τοῖς πράγμασιν ἀληθείας ἀπᾴδοντα, πῶς ἔτι δυνατὸν ἐν τοῖς ἐπιστήμοσιν καὶ τόνδε τὸν ποιητὴν καταλέγειν, καὶ ταῦτα τῆς περὶ τῶν θείων γενῶν καὶ τῶν ἀεὶ ὄντων διδασκαλίας· εἰ δὲ τά τε ἄλλα Ὁμήρῳ καὶ ταῦτα τῆς πρεπούσης ἠξίωται παραδόσεως, πῶς ἔτι κατὰ νοῦν τὸν Πλάτωνα καὶ τὴν ἀνέλεγκτον γνῶσιν ἐνεργεῖν συγχωρήσει τις; ἔστιν μὲν οὖν ὅπερ ἔφην καὶ ταῦτα σκέψεως δεόμενα, μάλιστα δὲ ἁπάντων ἐκεῖνο ἡμῖν δοκεῖ παμπόλλην ἐξέτασιν ἀπαιτεῖν, τὸ καὶ αὐτὸν τὸν Πλάτωνα πρὸς ἑαυτὸν ἐν τοῖς περὶ Ὁμήρου λόγοις διαμάχεσθαι. πῶς γὰρ ἂν ἀλλήλοις συμβαίνοιεν ὅ τε ἐν τῷ Φαίδωνι λεγόμενος παρ' αὐτῷ θεῖος ποιητὴς καὶ ὁ ἐν Πολιτείᾳ τρίτος ἀπὸ τῆς ἀληθείας δεικνύμενος;

ibid. 71.2-17

Φέρ' οὖν ὅσα κἀνταῦθα τοῦ καθηγεμόνος ἡμῶν ἠκούσαμεν περὶ τούτων διαταττομένου καὶ τῆς κοινωνίας τῶν δογμάτων, ἣν ἔχει τὰ Ὁμήρου ποιήματα πρὸς τὴν ὑπὸ τοῦ Πλάτωνος ἐν ὑστέροις χρόνοις καθεωραμένην ἀλήθειαν, συλλαβόντες ἐν τάξει διέλθωμεν καὶ θεωρήσωμεν πρῶτον μέν, εἴ πῃ δυνατὸν τὰς τοῦ Σωκράτους ἀπορίας διαλύειν· δεύτερον δὲ τὸν σκοπὸν τῆς φαινομένης ταύτης πρὸς Ὅμηρον ἀπαντήσεως· τρίτον δὲ αὖ τὴν τῶν Πλάτωνι δοκούντων περί τε ποιητικῆς αὐτῆς καὶ Ὁμήρου μίαν καὶ ἀνέλεγκτον ἀλήθειαν πανταχοῦ προβεβλημένην. οὕτω γὰρ ἂν ἑκάτερος ἡμῖν ἀποφανθείη τῶν θείων κατὰ νοῦν καὶ ἐπιστήμην θεωρὸς | καὶ περὶ τῶν αὐτῶν ἀμφότεροι τὰ αὐτὰ διδάσκοντες | καὶ ὡς ἀφ' ἑνὸς θεοῦ προεληλυθότες καὶ μίαν συμπληροῦντες σειράν, τῆς αὐτῆς περὶ τῶν ὄντων ἀληθείας ὑπάρχοντες ἐξηγηταί.

ibid. 73.11-22

οὐ γὰρ ἐοικότα φανεῖται τὰ σύμβολα ταῦτα ταῖς ὑπάρξεσι τῶν θεῶν. δεῖ δὲ ἄρα τοὺς μύθους, εἴπερ μὴ παντάπασιν ἀποπεπτωκότες ἔσονται τῆς ἐν τοῖς οὖσιν ἀληθείας, ἀπεικάζεσθαί πως τοῖς πράγμασιν, ὧν ἀποκρύπτειν τοῖς φαινομένοις παραπετάσμασιν τὴν θεωρίαν ἐπιχειροῦσιν. ἀλλ' ὥσπερ αὐτὸς ὁ Πλάτων πολλαχῇ διά τινων εἰκόνων | τὰ θεῖα μυστικῶς ἀναδιδάσκει, καὶ οὔτε αἶσχος οὐδὲν οὔτε ἀταξίας ἔμφασις οὔτε ἔνυλον καὶ ταραχῶδες φάντασμα παρεμπίπτει τοῖς μύθοις, ἀλλ' αὐτὰ τὰ περὶ θεῶν νοήματα ἄχραντα ἀποκέκρυπται, προβέβληνται δὲ αὐτῶν οἷον ἀγάλματα ἐμφανῆ τοῖς ἔνδον ἀπεικασμένα ὁμοιώματα τῆς ἀπορρήτου θεωρίας, . . .

ibid. 77.1-4

τὰς δὲ ἀνεγείρεσθαι πρὸς νοῦν δυναμένας καὶ πρὸς τὰ ὅλα γένη τῶν θεῶν καὶ τὰς διὰ πάντων προόδους τῶν ὄντων καὶ τὰς σειρὰς καὶ τὰς ἀποτελευτήσεις τὰς ἄχρι τῶν ἐσχάτων ἀνατείνεσθαι σπευδούσας.

ibid. 78.18-79.4

ὥσπερ οὖν ἡ τῶν ἱερῶν τέχνη κατανείμασα δεόντως τὴν σύμπασαν θρησκείαν τοῖς θεοῖς καὶ τοῖς τῶν θεῶν ὀπαδοῖς, ἵνα μηδὲν ἄμοιρον τῆς ἐπιβαλλούσης θεραπείας ἀπολείπηται τῶν ἀϊδίως ἑπομένων τοῖς θεοῖς, τοὺς μὲν ταῖς ἁγιωτάταις τελεταῖς καὶ τοῖς μυστικοῖς συμβόλοις προσάγεται, τῶν δὲ τοῖς φαινομένοις παθήμασιν προκαλεῖται τὰς δόσεις διὰ δή τινος ἀρρήτου συμπαθείας, οὕτως ἄρα καὶ οἱ τῶν τοιῶνδε μύθων πατέρες εἰς πᾶσαν ὡς εἰπεῖν ἀποβλέψαντες τὴν τῶν θείων πρόοδον καὶ τοὺς μύθους εἰς ὅλην ἀνάγειν σπεύδοντες τὴν ἀφ' ἑκάστου προϊοῦσαν σειρὰν | τὸ μὲν προβεβλημένον αὐτῶν καὶ εἰδωλικὸν ἀνάλογον ὑπεστήσαντο τοῖς ἐσχάτοις γένεσιν καὶ τῶν τελευταίων καὶ ἐνύλων προεστηκόσι παθῶν, τὸ δὲ ἀποκεκρυμμένον καὶ ἄγνωστον τοῖς πολλοῖς τῆς ἐν ἀβάτοις ἐξηρημένης τῶν θεῶν οὐσίας ἐκφαντικὸν τοῖς φιλοθεάμοσιν τῶν ὄντων παρέδοσαν. καὶ οὕτω δὴ τῶν μύθων ἕκαστος δαιμόνιος μέν ἐστι κατὰ τὸ φαινόμενον, θεῖος δὲ κατὰ τὴν ἀπόρρητον θεωρίαν.

ibid. 82.2-83.10

... οὔτε τὰς Ἡφαίστου ῥίψεις ἀπορήσομεν ἀνάγειν εἰς τὴν περὶ θεῶν ἀνέλεγκτον ἐπιστήμην οὔτε τοὺς Κρονίους δεσμοὺς οὔτε τὰς Οὐρανοῦ τομάς, ἃ δὴ ταῖς τῶν νέων ἀκοαῖς ἀσύμμετρά φησιν ὁ Σωκράτης ὑπάρχειν καὶ οὐδαμῶς συναρμόζεσθαι ταῖς ἕξεσιν τῶν παιδείας μόνης δεομένων· ὅλως γὰρ ἐν ἀλλοτρίαις ὑποδοχαῖς ἡ μυστικὴ τῶν θείων γνῶσις οὐκ ἄν ποτε ἐγγένοιτο. τούτοις δὴ οὖν τοῖς τῶν τοιῶνδε θεαμάτων ἐπιβόλοις λέγοντες, ὡς ἄρα ἡ μὲν Ἡφαίστου ῥῖψις τὴν ἄνωθεν ἄχρι τῶν τελευταίων ἐν τοῖς αἰσθητοῖς δημιουργημάτων τοῦ θείου πρόοδον ἐνδείκνυται, κινουμένην καὶ τελειουμένην καὶ ποδηγετουμένην ὑπὸ τοῦ πάντων δημιουργοῦ καὶ πατρός, οἱ δὲ Κρό|νιοι δεσμοὶ τὴν ἕνωσιν τῆς ὅλης δημιουργίας πρὸς τὴν νοερὰν τοῦ Κρόνου καὶ πατρικὴν ὑπεροχὴν δηλοῦσιν, αἱ δὲ τοῦ Οὐρανοῦ τομαὶ τὴν διάκρισιν τῆς Τιτανικῆς σειρᾶς ἀπὸ τῆς συνεκτικῆς διακοσμήσεως αἰνίσσονται, τάχα ἂν γνώριμα λέγοιμεν καὶ τὸ τῶν μύθων τραγικὸν καὶ πλασματῶδες εἰς τὴν νοερὰν τῶν θείων γενῶν ἀναπέμποιμεν θεωρίαν. πάντα γὰρ τὰ παρ' ἡμῖν κατὰ τὸ χεῖρον ἐμφανταζόμενα καὶ τῆς καταδεεστέρας ὄντα συστοιχίας ἐπ' ἐκείνων οἱ μῦθοι κατ' αὐτὴν τὴν κρείττονα φύσιν καὶ δύναμιν παραλαμβάνουσιν. οἷον ὁ δεσμὸς παρ' ἡμῖν μὲν κώλυσίς ἐστι καὶ ἐπίσχεσις τῆς ἐνεργείας, ἐκεῖ δὲ συναφὴ πρὸς τὰ αἴτια καὶ ἕνωσις ἄρρητος. καὶ ἡ ῥῖψις ἐνταῦθα μὲν κίνησίς ἐστι βίαιος ὑπ' ἄλλου, παρὰ δὲ τοῖς θεοῖς τὴν γόνιμον ἐνδείκνυται πρόοδον καὶ τὴν ἄφετον ἐπὶ πάντα παρουσίαν καὶ εὔλυτον, οὐκ ἀφισταμένην τῆς οἰκείας ἀρχῆς, ἀλλ' ἀπ' ἐκείνης διὰ πάντων ἐν τάξει προϊοῦσαν. καὶ αἱ τομαὶ τοῖς μὲν μεριστοῖς πράγμασιν καὶ ἐνύλοις ἐλάττωσιν ἐμποιοῦσιν τῆς δυνάμεως, ἐν δὲ ταῖς πρωτουργοῖς αἰτίαις πρόοδον τῶν δευτέρων εἰς ὑφειμένην τάξιν ἀπὸ τῶν σφετέρων αἰτίων αἰνίσσονται, τῶν πρώτων ἀνελαττώτων ἐν ἑαυτοῖς ἱδρυμένων, καὶ μήτε κινουμένων ἀφ' ἑαυτῶν διὰ τὴν τούτων πρόοδον μήτε ἐλασσουμένων διὰ τὸν τούτων χωρισμὸν μήτε διαιρουμένων διὰ τὴν ἐν τοῖς καταδεεστέροις διάκρισιν. ἀλλὰ ταῦτα καὶ ὁ Σωκράτης φησὶν νέοις μὲν ἀνεπιτήδεια ἀκούειν, τοῖς δὲ ἐν ἀπορρήτῳ τὴν περὶ θεῶν ἀλήθειαν συναιρεῖν ἀπὸ τῶν μυθικῶν συμβόλων δυναμένοις ζητεῖν τε καὶ θεάσασθαι προσήκει·

ibid. 83.12-22

πέπονθεν γὰρ τοῦτο καὶ ταῦτα τὰ μυθικὰ πλάσματα, ὅπερ ὁ Πλάτων πού φησι τὰ θεῖα καὶ παναγέστατα τῶν δογμάτων πεπονθέναι. καὶ γὰρ ταῦτα τοῖς μὲν πολλοῖς ἐστι καταγέλαστα, τοῖς δὲ εἰς νοῦν ἀνεγειρομένοις ὀλίγοις δή τισιν ἐκφαίνει τὴν ἑαυτῶν πρὸς τὰ πράγματα συμπάθειαν, καὶ τὴν ἐξ αὐτῶν τῶν ἱερατικῶν ἔργων παρέχεται πίστιν τῆς πρὸς τὰ θεῖα συμφυοῦς δυνάμεως· καὶ γὰρ οἱ θεοὶ τῶν τοιῶνδε συμβόλων ἀκούοντες χαίρουσιν καὶ τοῖς καλοῦσιν ἑτοίμως πείθονται καὶ τὴν ἑαυτῶν ἰδιότητα προφαίνουσιν διὰ τούτων ὡς οἰκείων αὐτοῖς καὶ μάλιστα γνωρίμων συνθημάτων·

ibid. 83.26-84.12

μὴ τοίνυν λέγωμεν ὡς οὐ παιδευτικοὶ πρὸς ἀρετήν εἰσιν οἱ τοιοίδε μῦθοι τῶν παρ' Ἕλλησιν θεολόγων, ἀλλ' ὡς οὐχὶ τοῖς ἱερατικοῖς θεσμοῖς συμφωνότατοι δεικνύωμεν, μηδὲ ὡς ἀνομοίως μιμοῦνται τὰ θεῖα διὰ τῶν ἀπεμφαινόντων συμβόλων, ἀλλ' ὡς οὐχὶ συμπάθειαν ἡμῖν ἄρρητον προπαρασκευάζουσιν εἰς τὴν μετουσίαν τῶν θεῶν. οἱ μὲν γὰρ εἰς τὴν τῶν | νέων παιδείαν συντείνοντες ἔστωσαν πολὺ μὲν τὸ εἰκὸς ἔχοντες, πολλὴν δὲ τὴν ἐν τοῖς φαινομένοις τύποις τῆς μυθοποιίας εὐπρέπειαν, πάντη δὲ τῶν ἐναντίων ὀνομάτων καθαρεύοντες καὶ δι' ὁμοιότητος τῶν συμβόλων πρὸς τὰ θεῖα συνάπτοντες, οἱ δὲ ἐνθεαστικωτέρας στοχαζόμενοι ἕξεως καὶ δι' ἀναλογίας μόνης τὰ ἔσχατα τοῖς πρωτίστοις συναρμόζοντες καὶ τῆς ἐν τῷ παντὶ συμπαθείας τῶν ἀποτελεσμάτων πρὸς τὰ γεννητικὰ αὐτῶν αἴτια ποιούμενοι τὸν σύμπαντα λόγον εἰκότως δήπου τῶν πολλῶν ἡμῶν ὑπεριδόντες χρῶνται παντοίως τοῖς ὀνόμασιν εἰς τὴν τῶν θείων πραγμάτων ἔνδειξιν.

ibid. 85.16-86.23

δοκεῖ δέ μοι καὶ τὸ τῶν ποιητικῶν πλασμάτων τραγικὸν καὶ τὸ τερατῶδες καὶ τὸ παρὰ φύσιν κινεῖν τοὺς ἀκούοντας παντοδαπῶς εἰς τὴν τῆς ἀληθείας ζήτησιν καὶ εἶναι πρὸς τὴν ἀπόρρητον γνῶσιν ὁλκὸν καὶ μὴ ἐπιτρέπειν ἡμῖν διὰ τὴν φαι|νομένην πιθανότητα μένειν ἐπὶ τῶν προβεβλημένων ἐννοιῶν, ἀλλ' ἀναγκάζειν εἰς τὸ ἐντὸς τῶν μύθων διαβάλλειν καὶ τὸν κεκρυμμένον ἐν ἀφανεῖ τῶν μυθοπλαστῶν περιεργάζεσθαι νοῦν, καὶ θεωρεῖν ὁποίας μὲν φύσεις, ἡλίκας δὲ δυνάμεις ἐκεῖνοι λαβόντες εἰς τὴν αὐτῶν διάνοιαν τοῖσδε τοῖς συμβόλοις αὐτὰς τοῖς μεθ' ἑαυτοὺς ἐσήμηναν. ὅτε τοίνυν ἀνεγείρουσιν μὲν οἱ τοιοίδε μῦθοι τοὺς εὐφυεστέρους πρὸς τὴν ἔφεσιν τῆς ἐν αὐτοῖς ἀποκρύφου θεωρίας καὶ διὰ τὴν φαινομένην τερατολογίαν τῆς ἐν τοῖς ἀδύτοις ἱδρυμένης ἀληθείας ἀνακινοῦσιν τὴν ζήτησιν, τοῖς δὲ βεβήλοις ὧν μὴ θέμις αὐτοῖς <οὐ> συγχωροῦσιν ἐφάπτεσθαι, πῶς οὐ διαφερόντως ἂν προσήκοιεν τοῖς θεοῖς αὐτοῖς, ὧν εἰσιν ἐξηγηταὶ τῆς ὑποστάσεως; καὶ γὰρ τῶν θεῶν πολλὰ προβέβληται γένη, τὰ μὲν τῆς δαιμονίας τάξεως, τὰ δὲ τῆς ἀγγελικῆς, καταπλήττοντα τοὺς εἰς τὴν μετουσίαν αὐτῶν ἐγειρομένους καὶ γυμναζομένους πρὸς τὴν τοῦ φωτὸς καταδοχὴν καὶ εἰς ὕψος ἐπαίροντα πρὸς τὴν ἕνωσιν τῶν θεῶν. μάλιστα δ' ἄν τις κατίδοι τὴν τῶν μύθων τούτων πρὸς τὸ τῶν δαιμόνων φῦλον συγγένειαν καὶ διὰ τῆς ἐκείνων ἐνεργείας συμβολικῶς τὰ πολλὰ δηλούσης, οἷον εἴ τινες ἡμῶν ὕπαρ ἐγένοντο δαίμοσιν προστυχεῖς ἢ καὶ ὄναρ τῆς παρ' αὐτῶν ἀπολελαύκασιν ἐπιπνοίας πολλὰ τῶν γενομένων ἢ καὶ ἐσομένων ἐκφαινούσης. ἐν πάσαις γὰρ ταῖς τοιαύταις φαντασίαις κατὰ τοὺς μυθοπλάστας ἄλλα ἐξ ἄλλων ἐνδείκνυται, καὶ οὐ τὰ μὲν | εἰκόνες, τὰ δὲ παραδείγματα, ὅσα διὰ τούτων σημαίνουσιν, ἀλλὰ τὰ μὲν σύμβολα, τὰ δὲ ἐξ ἀναλογίας ἔχει τὴν πρὸς ταῦτα συμπάθειαν. εἰ τοίνυν δαιμόνιος ὁ τρόπος ἐστὶ τῆς τοιαύτης μυθοποιίας, πῶς οὐ πάντῃ φήσομεν αὐτὸν ἐξῃρῆσθαι τῆς ἄλλης ἁπάσης τῶν μύθων ποικιλίας, τῆς τε εἰς τὴν φύσιν βλεπούσης καὶ τὰς φυσικὰς δυνάμεις ἀφερμηνευούσης, καὶ τῆς τὰ ἤθη τῶν ψυχῶν παιδεύειν προστησαμένης;

ibid. 159.10-22

Εἰ δὲ τοῖς ὑπ' αὐτῷ νομοθέτῃ τρεφομένοις καὶ κατὰ τὸ πρώτιστον εἶδος τῆς ζωῆς τελειουμένοις ἄβατόν τε τὴν ψυχὴν ἔχειν ὀφείλουσιν ἁπάσης ποικιλίας καὶ τῆς ἐναντίας διαθέσεως τῷ καλῷ ⟨καὶ⟩ τῷ ἀγαθῷ καὶ πρὸς μόνον τὸν τῆς ἀρετῆς ὅρον ἀποβλέπειν ἀνάρμοστός ἐστιν ἡ τοιαύτη διδασκαλία, τῆς μὲν ἁπλότητος τῶν θείων πολυειδῆ παραπετάσματα μηχανησαμένη, τῆς δὲ ὑπερφυοῦς περὶ αὐτῶν ἀληθείας καὶ τῆς ἐπέκεινα τῶν καλῶν πάντων ὑπάρξεως τὰ φαινόμενα αἰσχρὰ καὶ τὰ παρὰ φύσιν προκαλύμματα ποιησαμένη, πῶς διὰ ταῦτα προσήκει τὴν Ὁμηρικὴν θεωρίαν διοικίζειν τῆς Πλατωνικῆς φιλοσοφίας, εἰ μὴ καὶ τὴν αὐτοῦ τοῦ Πλάτωνος πραγματείαν διιστάνειν τῆς Πλάτωνος ἐπιστήμης ἀνεξόμεθα;

ibid. 162.3-19

τῷ γὰρ ἁπλῷ τὸ ποικίλον, καὶ τῷ μονοειδεῖ τὸ πολυειδές, καὶ τῷ παραδείγματι τῆς ἀρίστης ζωῆς τὸ μιμητικὸν γένος οὐκ ἄν ποτε προσαρμοσθείη· παράδειγμα δέ, φησὶν ὁ Σωκράτης, πολιτείας ὀρθῆς καὶ τελέας γράφομεν. διὸ καὶ πάντα αὐτῇ πρὸς ἀκρίβειαν τὰ ἀγαθὰ φέροντες ἀποδίδομεν, τὴν ἕνωσιν, τὴν ἁπλότητα, τὴν ἀλήθειαν, τὴν αὐτάρκειαν. ὥσπερ οὖν εἴ τις τοῖς νοητοῖς εἴδεσιν, ἃ δὴ παραδείγματα τῶν ὄντων εἶναι τιθέμεθα, σχῆμα προσάγοι καὶ μέγεθος καὶ χρόαν, καὶ ὅσα ἄλλα προσήκει ταῖς τούτων εἰκόσιν, ἀλλ' οὐ τοῖς πρωτουργοῖς καὶ ὄντως οὖσιν γένεσιν, συγχεῖν αὐτὸν ⟨τὰ⟩ κατ' οὐσίαν διεστῶτα καὶ συγκλώθειν τὰ ἀνάρμοστά φαμεν, οὕτως οἶμαι καὶ τοῖς ἐν τῇ τελεωτάτῃ πολιτείᾳ φῦσίν τε καὶ

τρεφομένοις ἤθεσιν καὶ κατα τὸ παράδειγμα τῆς ἀρίστης παιδείας τελειουμένοις μιμήσεις διὰ λόγων καὶ εἴδη παντοίας ζωῆς καὶ σκηνὴν τῶν δια-
φόρων παθημάτων ‹τῶν› ἐν τοῖς ἀνθρώποις προτείνειν οὐκ ἄν ποτε συγχω-
ρήσαιμεν.

ibid. 198.8-24

Τί οὖν ταῦτα πρὸς τὴν καθ' Ὅμηρον ποιητικήν; πρὸς μὲν γὰρ τὴν
τραγικὴν ποίησιν καὶ κωμικὴν ἱκανά· τούτων γὰρ τὸ ὅλον μίμησίς ἐστιν
πρὸς τὴν τῶν ἀκουόντων ἐξειργασμένη ψυχαγωγίαν· πρὸς δὲ τὴν Ὁμήρου |
ποιητικὴν τὴν ἀπὸ θεῶν ὡρμημένην καὶ τῶν ὄντων ἐκφαίνουσαν τὴν φύσιν
οὐδὲν ἂν προσήκοι. καὶ πῶς γὰρ ἂν ἡ διὰ συμβόλων τὰ θεῖα ἀφερμηνεύουσα
μιμητικὴ προσαγορεύοιτο; τὰ γὰρ σύβολα τούτων, ὧν ἐστι σύμβολα, μιμήματα οὐκ ἔστιν· τὰ μὲν γὰρ ἐναντία τῶν ἐναντίων οὐκ ἄν ποτε μιμήματα
γένοιτο, τοῦ καλοῦ τὸ αἰσχρόν, καὶ τοῦ κατὰ φύσιν τὸ παρὰ φύσιν· ἡ δὲ
συμβολικὴ θεωρία καὶ διὰ τῶν ἐναντιωτάτων τὴν τῶν πραγμάτων ἐνδεί-
κνυται φύσιν. εἴ τις ἄρα ποιητὴς ἔνθους ἐστὶν καὶ διὰ συνθημάτων δηλοῖ
τὴν περὶ τῶν ὄντων ἀλήθειαν, ἢ εἴ τις ἐπιστήμη χρώμενος αὐτὴν ἡμῖν
ἐκφαίνει τὴν τάξιν τῶν πραγμάτων, οὗτος οὔτε μιμητής ἐστιν οὔτε ἐλέγχε-
σθαι δύναται διὰ τῶν προκειμένων ἀποδείξεων.

Proclus, *In Timaeum*, vol. I. 1.4-8

Ὅτι μὲν ἡ τοῦ Πλατωνικοῦ Τιμαίου πρόθεσις τῆς ὅλης φυσιολογίας ἀντέχεται καὶ ὡς πρὸς τὴν τοῦ παντὸς ἀνήκει θεωρίαν, ἐξ ἀρχῆς εἰς
τέλος τοῦτο πραγματευομένου, τοῖς μὴ παντάπασιν ἐσκοτωμένοις πρὸς
τοὺς λόγους ἐναργὲς εἶναί μοι καταφαίνεται.

ibid. 15.22-25

χαρίεντα μὲν οὖν πάντα ταῦτα καὶ ὅσα τοιαῦτα ἄν τις ἐπινοήσειεν εἰς
θεωρίαν τῆς προκειμένης ῥήσεως· δεῖ δὲ μεμνῆσθαι καὶ ὅτι Πυθαγόρειος
ὁ διάλογος, καὶ χρὴ τὸν προσήκοντα τρόπον ἐκείνοις ποιεῖσθαι τὰς ἐξηγή-
σεις.

ibid. 19.22-29

λέγει δὴ οὖν ὁ λόγος τὸν ἀπολειπόμενον ὡς ἀσύμμετρον τοῖς φυσικοῖς
λόγοις ἀπεῖναι, βούλεσθαι δ' ἂν παρεῖναι τούτοις, εἰ περὶ τὰ νοητὰ δια-
τρίψειν ἔμελλον. καὶ σχεδὸν ἅπαντα τὰ πρὸ τῆς φυσιολογίας ὁ μὲν ἐξηγεῖ-
ται πολιτικώτερον, ὁ Πορφύριος, εἰς τὰς ἀρετὰς ἀναφέρων καὶ τὰ λεγό-
μενα καθήκοντα, ὁ δὲ φυσικώτερον· δεῖν γὰρ τῷ προκειμένῳ σκοπῷ πάντα
σύμφωνα εἶναι· φυσικὸς δὲ ὁ διάλογος, ἀλλ' οὐκ ἠθικός.

ibid. 30.11-18

κἀνταῦθα τοίνυν ἡ μὲν τῆς πολιτείας πρὸ τῆς φυσιολογίας ἐπιτετμημένη παράδοσις εἰκονικῶς ἡμᾶς ἐφίστησι τῇ δημιουργίᾳ τοῦ παντός, ἡ δὲ περὶ τῶν Ἀτλαντίνων ἱστορία συμβολικῶς· καὶ γὰρ οἱ μῦθοι τὰ πολλὰ διὰ τῶν συμβόλων εἰώθασι τὰ πράγματα ἐνδείκνυσθαι· ὥστε εἶναι τὸ φυσιολογικὸν διὰ παντὸς τοῦ διαλόγου διῆκον, ἀλλ' οὗ μὲν ἄλλως οὗ δὲ ἄλλως κατὰ τοὺς διαφόρους τρόπους τῆς παραδόσεως.

ibid. 60.4-11

καὶ ἡμεῖς δὲ φαῖμεν ἂν καὶ τὴν παραβολὴν ταύτην παρειλῆφθαι, διότι καὶ ἡ πολιτεία καθ' ὁμοίωσιν ἀναγέγραπται τῶν θείων, καὶ τὴν χάριν τῶν ὀνομάτων εἰκόνα φέρειν τῆς ὑπὸ τοῦ δημιουργοῦ τοῖς οὐρανίοις ἐνδοθείσης χάριτος, καὶ τὸ τεχνικὸν τῆς ἑρμηνείας τῷ αὐτοφυεῖ συγκεκραμένον ἀπεικονίζεσθαι τὴν θείαν ποίησιν, ἔχουσαν μὲν καὶ τὸν ἀφ' ἑαυτῆς ὅρον, ἔχουσαν δὲ καὶ τὸ ἀπὸ τοῦ εἶναι καὶ τῆς οὐσίας προϊόν.

ibid. 87.6-15

ὁ δὲ δὴ μέγας Ἰάμβλιχος ἀξιοῖ μᾶλλον ἡμᾶς ἐπὶ τὰ πράγματα τῶν λόγων τὴν ποικιλίαν ἀνάγειν καὶ ὁρᾶν, ὅπως καὶ ἐν τῇ φύσει τὰ ἐναντία τῷ ἑνὶ κεκράτηται, καὶ τὸ ἓν ὅπως ποικίλλεται, καὶ οἱ αὐτοὶ λόγοι πόσην ἐξαλλαγὴν ἐπιφαίνουσιν, ἄλλως μὲν ὄντες ἐν τῷ νῷ τοῦ παντός, ἄλλως δὲ ἐν τῇ ψυχῇ καὶ ἄλλως ἐν τῇ φύσει καὶ ἐσχάτως ἐν ὕλῃ γεγονότες καὶ αὖ περὶ τὴν ὕλην μετὰ τῆς ὁμοιότητος παμπόλλην τὴν ἑτερότητα δεικνύντες· ταῦτα γάρ ἐστιν ἐπάξια τῆς τοῦ Πλάτωνος διανοίας, ἀλλ' οὐχ ἡ πολυπραγμοσύνη τῆς λέξεως.

ibid. 132.21-27

ὃ καὶ ὁ Πλάτων εἰδὼς διὰ συμβόλων καὶ αἰνιγμάτων τὴν ἐναντίωσιν ἡμῖν παραδίδωσι τῶν ἐν τῷ παντὶ γενῶν ἥτις ἐστί, καὶ ὅπως διὰ τὴν νοερὰν ἐνέργειαν τῆς Ἀθηνᾶς καθυποτάττεται τὰ χείρω τοῖς ἀμείνοσιν. εἰκότως ἄρα καὶ ἔργα τῶν Ἀθηναίων καὶ πολιτείας ἐκάλεσεν ὁ Πλάτων, ὅτι διὰ πάντων ᾔδει χωροῦσαν τὴν τοιαύτην ἀναλογίαν,

Proclus, *In Timaeum*, vol. II.23.9-16

Μετὰ δὴ τὴν μαθηματικὴν ἀνάληψιν τῶν ῥημάτων τούτων ἐπὶ τὴν φυσικὴν δεῖ τρέπεσθαι θεωρίαν. οὔτε γὰρ τοῖς μαθήμασιν ἐγκαταμένειν προσήκει τὸν λόγον ἀπαρτῶντας (φυσικὸς γὰρ ὁ διάλογος) οὔτε ἀμελεῖν τῶν λόγων ἐκείνων τὸ πρὸς αἴσθησιν μόνον ἐπιζητοῦντας, ἀλλὰ δεῖ συνάπτειν ἀμφότερα καὶ συμπλέκειν ἀεὶ τὰ φυσικὰ τοῖς μαθηματικοῖς, ὥσπερ καὶ αὐτὰ τὰ πράγματα συμπλέκεται καὶ ἔστιν ὁμογενῆ καὶ ἀδελφὰ κατὰ τὴν ἀπὸ νοῦ πρόοδον.

ibid. 36.20-27

'Απὸ δὲ τούτων ὁρμηθέντες κατίδωμεν, ὅπως καὶ τὰ φυσικὰ διανοήματα σύμφωνα τούτοις ἐστί, καὶ τοῖς ἐπιστημονικοῖς λόγοις τοὺς εἰκότας συναρμόσωμεν, καὶ πρῶτον, τί τὸ ἐπίπεδον τὸ φυσικόν, καὶ πῶς ἐπὶ τούτων μία μεσότης, δύο δὲ ἐπ' αὐτῶν τῶν στερεοειδῶν. ὁ μὲν θεῖος Ἰάμβλιχος — οὗτος γὰρ ὁ ἀνὴρ διαφερόντως ἀντελάβετο τῆς τοιαύτης θεωρίας, τῶν ἄλλων ὥσπερ καθευδόντων καὶ περὶ τὸ μαθηματικὸν καλινδουμένων μόνον — . . .

BIBLIOGRAPHY

I. WORKS OF THE NEOPLATONISTS

A. *Commentaries*

1. *Editions of the Greek texts*

Damascius, *Lectures on the Philebus, Wrongly Attributed to Olympiodorus.* Text, translation, notes and indices by L. G. Westerink (Amsterdam, 1959).

Hermeias Alexandrinus, *In Platonis Phaedrum Scholia*, ed. P. Couvreur (Paris, 1901; reprint Hildesheim, 1971).

Iamblichus Chalcidensis, *In Platonis dialogos commentariorum fragmenta*, edited with translation and commentary by J. M. Dillon (*Philosophia antiqua*, 23 [Leiden, 1973]).

Olympiodorus, *Commentary on the First Alcibiades of Plato*, Critical text and indices by L. G. Westerink (Amsterdam, 1956).

——, *In Platonis Gorgiam Commentaria*, ed. L. G. Westerink (Leipzig, 1970).

——, *In Platonis Phaedonem Commentaria*, ed. W. Norvin (Leipzig, 1913; reprint Hildesheim, 1968).

Proclus Diadochus, *Commentary on the First Alcibiades of Plato*, Critical text and indices by L. G. Westerink (Amsterdam, 1954).

——, *In Platonis Cratylum Commentaria*, ed. G. Pasquali (Leipzig, 1908).

——, *Commentarium in Platonis Parmenidem*, ed. V. Cousin (Paris, 1864; reprint Hildesheim, 1961).

——, *In Platonis Rem Publicam Commentarii*, 2 vols., ed. W. Kroll (Leipzig, 1899-1901; reprint Amsterdam, 1965).

——, *In Platonis Timaeum Commentaria*, 3 vols., ed. E. Diehl (Leipzig, 1903-1906; reprint Amsterdam, 1965).

2. *Modern translations of the Neoplatonic commentaries*

Proclus, *Alcibiades I*, translation and commentary by W. O'Neill (The Hague, 1965).

——, *Commentaire sur le Parménide*, 3 vols., translated by A. Ed. Chaignet (Paris, 1900-1903; reprint Frankfort a.M., 1962).

——, *Commentaire sur la République*, 3 vols., translated by A. J. Festugière (Paris, 1970).

——, *Commentaire sur le Timée*, 5 vols., translated by A. J. Festugière (Paris, 1966-1968).

B. *Other works*

Anonymous Prolegomena to Platonic Philosophy, Introduction, text, translation and indices by L. G. Westerink (Amsterdam, 1962).

Porphyry, *The Cave of the Nymphs*, ed. L. Westerink and others (*Arethusa Monograph*, I [Buffalo, 1969]).

Proclus, *Elements of Theology* [2], ed. E. R. Dodds (Oxford, 1963).

Proclus, *La théologie Platonicienne*, Book I, ed. H. D. Saffrey and L. G. Westerink (Paris, Budé, 1968).

II. EDITIONS AND TRANSLATIONS OF ANCIENT AUTHORS

Aeschylus, *Agamemnon*, 3 vols., ed. Ed. Fraenkel (Oxford, 1950).
Aristotle, *Poetics*, ed. D. W. Lucas (Oxford, 1968).
Aristotle, *The Rhetoric of Aristotle*, tr. L. Cooper (New York, 1932; and paperback reprint).
Dionysius of Halicarnassus, *Opuscula*, 2 vols. (Leipzig, 1899-1929, repr, 1965).
Ps.-Heraclitus, *Allegories d'Homère*, ed. F. Buffière (Paris, Budé, 1962).
Plato, *Timaeus*, tr. F. Cornford, in *Plato's Cosmology* (London, 1937 and paperback reprints).
——, *The Republic*, tr. H. D. P. Lee (Baltimore, Penguin Books, 1955).
Plutarch, *How the Young Man Should Study Poetry*, tr. Babbit, *Moralia*, vol. 1 (Cambridge, Mass., Loeb Library, 1927 and subsequent reprints).
Seneca, *Epistulae Morales*, vol. 1, tr. R. M. Gummere (Cambridge, U.S.A., Loeb Library, 1917 and reprints).
Stoicorum Veterum Fragmenta (Leipzig, 1903), vol. 2, ed. H. von Arnim.

II. MODERN SCHOLARLY LITERATURE

von Albrecht, M. 'Allegorie,' *Lexikon der alten Welt* (Zurich, 1965), 121-124.
Allen, D. C. *Mysteriously Meant* (Baltimore, 1970).
Allers, R. 'Microcosmos from Anaximandros to Paracelsus,' *Traditio* 2 (1944), 319-409.
Altman, A. 'Bible: Allegorical Interpretations,' *Encyclopedia Judaica*, vol. 3 (Jerusalem, 1971), 895-899.
Baldwin, C. S. *Ancient Rhetoric and Poetic* (New York, 1924).
Beutler, R. 'Proklos,' *RE* 23 (1957), 186-247.
Bielmeier, A. *Die neuplatonischen Phaidrosenterpretationen* (*Rhetorische Studien*, Heft 16) (Paderborn, 1930).
Boas, G. 'Macrocosm and Microcosm,' *Dictionary of the History of Ideas*, vol. 3, ed. Ph. Wiener (New York, 1973), 126-131.
Bonner, S. F. *The Literary Treatises of Dionysius of Halicarnassus* (Cambridge, 1939; reprint 1969).
Buffière, F. *Les mythes d'Homère et la pensée grecque* (Paris, 1956).
The Cambridge History of Later Greek and Early Medieval Philosophy, ed. A. H. Armstrong (Cambridge, 1967).
Clark, D. L. *Rhetoric in Greco-Roman Education* (New York, 1957).
Cornford, F. *From Religion to Philosophy* (London, 1912; paperback reprint 1957).
——. *Principium Sapientiae* (Cambridge, 1952; paperback reprint 1965).
Dodds, E. R., *The Greeks and the Irrational* (Berkeley, 1951).
——. *Pagan and Christian in an Age of Anxiety* (Cambridge, 1965).
Dornseiff, F. *Das Alphabet in Mystik und Magie* [2] (Leipzig, 1925).
Dörrie, H. 'Zur Methodik antiker Exegese,' *Zeitschrift für die neutestamentliche Wissenschaft* 65 (1974), 121-138.
Eberhardt, A. 'Vir Bonus Quadrato Lapidi Comparatur,' *Harvard Theological Review* 38 (1945), 177-193.
Edelstein, L. 'The function of the myth in Plato's philosophy,' *Journal of the History of Ideas* 10 (1949), 463-481.
Festugière, A. J. 'Modes des compositions des Commentaires de Proclus,' *Museum Helveticum* 20 (1963), 77-100.
——. *La Révélation d'Hermès Trismégiste*, vol. 3, *Le Dieu Cosmique* (Paris, 1949).

Fletcher, A., 'Allegory,' *Dictionary of the History of Ideas*, vol. 1, ed. Ph. Wiener (New York, 1968), 41-48.

Friedl, A. *Die Homer-Interpretationen des Neuplatonikers Proklos* (Diss., Würzburg, 1936).

Friedländer, P., *Plato*, vol. 1, tr. H. Meyerhoff (New York, 1958; paperback reprint 1964), 108-210.

Frye, N. 'Allegory,' *The Princeton Encyclopedia of Poetry and Poetics*, ed. A. Preminger (Princeton, 1965), 12-15.

——. *Anatomy of Criticism* (Princeton, 1957; paperback reprint 1965).

——. *A Natural Perspective* (New York, 1965).

Gallavotti, C. 'L'estetica greca nell'ultimo suo cultore,' *Memorie della R. Accademia delle Scienze di Torino*, Serie II, Vol. LXVII, N. 2, *Classe di Scienze morali, storiche e filologiche*.

——. 'Eterogeneità e cronologia dei commenti di Proclo alla *Repubblica*,' *Rivista di filologia*, 57, n.s. 7 (1929), 208-219.

Galli, V. 'La mimesi artistica secondo Aristotele' *Studi Italiani di Filologia Classica*, N.S., 4 (1926), 281-390.

Gombrich, E. H. J. *Symbolic Images. Studies in the Art of the Renaissance* (London, 1972).

Grube, G. M. A., *The Greek and Roman Critics* (London, 1965).

Havelock, E. *Preface to Plato* (Cambridge, U.S.A., 1963; paperback reprint 1967).

Hirzel, R. *Der Dialog* (Leipzig, 1895; reprint, 1963).

Hopfner, Th. 'Mageia' *RE* XIV (1930), 302-393.

——. 'Theurgie,' *RE* VI, 2nd ser. (1937), 258-270.

Kaufmann, J., 'Allegorie,' *Encyclopedia Judaica*, vol. 2 (Berlin, 1928), 335-338.

Kennedy, George. *The Art of Persuasion in Greece* (Princeton, 1963).

——. *The Art of Rhetoric in the Roman World* (Princeton, 1972).

Koller, H. *Mimesis in der Antike* (Bern, 1954).

Ladner, G. 'The Concept of the Image in the Church Fathers,' *Dumbarton Oaks Papers* 7 (1953), 1-34.

Lausberg, Heinrich. *Handbuch der literarischen Rhetorik*, 2 vols. (Munich, 1960).

Lidell and Scott. *Greek-English Lexicon*. New edition, revised by H. Stuart Jones (Oxford, 1940).

Lloyd, G. E. R. 'Analogy in Early Greek Thought,' *Dictionary of the History of Ideas*, vol. I, ed. Ph. Wiener (New York, 1968), 60-63.

McCall, M., Jr. *Ancient Rhetorical Theories of Simile and Comparison* (Cambridge, U.S.A., 1969).

McKeon, R. 'Literary criticism and the concept of imitation in antiquity,' *Modern Philology*, 34 (1936), 1-35, reprinted in *Critics and Criticism*, ed. R. Crane (Chicago, 1952).

Merki, H. 'Ebenbildlichkeit,' *Reallexikon für Antike und Christentum*, 4 (1959), 464-478.

Morrow, G. *Plato's Cretan City* (Princeton, 1960).

Müri, W. Σύμβολον (Bern, 1931).

Nahm, Milton. *The Artist as Creator* (Baltimore, 1956).

Nilsson, M. *Geschichte der griechischen Religion* [2], vol. 2 (Munich, 1961).

Nock, A. D. 'Kornutos,' *RE*, Supplbd. V (1931), 995-1005.

Panofsky, E. *Idea; ein Beitrag zur Begriffsgeschichte der älteren Kunsttheorie* [2] (Berlin, 1960).

Pépin, J. *Mythe et allégorie* (Paris, 1958).

——. 'Porphyre, exégète d'Homère,' *Entretiens sur l'antiquité classique*, XII. *Porphyre* (Geneva, 1965).

——. 'Remarques sur la théorie d'exégèse allégorique chez Philon,' *Philon d'Alexandrie* (Paris, Editions du Centre National de la Recherche Scientifique, 1967).

Praechter, K. 'Richtungen und Schulen in Neuplatonismus,' *Genethliakon Carl Robert* (Berlin, 1910), 105-156.

——. 'Syrianos' *RE* 4, 2nd ser. (1932), 1728-1775.

Reinhardt, K. *Kosmos und Sympathie* (Munich, 1926).

Roemer, Adolf. *Die Homerexegese Aristarchs* (Paderborn, 1924).

Roques, R. 'Dionysius Areopagita,' *Reallexikon für Antike und Christentum* 3 (1957), 1075-1121.

Rosán, L. J. *The Philosophy of Proclus* (New York, 1949).

Saxl, F. 'Macrocosm and Microcosm in Medieval Pictures,' *Lectures*, vol. 1 (London, 1957), 58-72.

——. *Die Vorbereitung des Neuplatonismus* (Berlin, 1930).

Tigerstedt, E. N. *Plato's Idea of Poetical Inspiration* (*Commentationes Humanarum Litt., Societas Scientiarum Fennica*, vol. 44) (Helsinki, 1969).

Verdenius, W. J. *Mimesis* (Leiden, 1949).

Volkmann, R. *Die Rhetorik der Griechen und Römer in systematischer Übersicht dargestellt* ² (Leipzig, 1874).

Wallis, R. T. *Neoplatonism* (London, 1972).

Waszink, J. 'Allegorese,' *Reallexikon für Antike und Christentum* vol. 1 (Stuttgart, 1950), 283-293.

Wellek, R. 'Symbol and Symbolism in Literature,' *Dictionary of the History of Ideas*, vol. 4, ed. Ph. Wiener (New York, 1973), 337-345.

Werner, J. 'Allegorische Dichtererklärung,' *Der Kleine Pauly*, vol. 2 (Stuttgart, 1964), 274.

Whittaker, Th. *The Neo-Platonists* ² (Cambridge, 1928).

Wind, E. *Pagan Mysteries in the Renaissance* ² (London, 1967).

INDEX OF PASSAGES

Anonymous

Anonymous Prolegomena to Platonic Philosophy
ed. Westerink, 15.1-7   101-102
— 16.1-6   102-103
— 16.7-8   120
— 20.9-12   122
— 21.2-28   82-84

Aristophanes

— *Frogs* 759-760   13
— 771-778   13

Aristotle

Poetics 1457b17-34   71
Rhetoric III.1404b8-12   18
— III.1405a10-14   18

Cicero

Orator 8-10   99

Cleanthes

Stoicorum Veterum Fragmenta, ed. v. Arnim
vol. 2, 256.14   64-65

Demetrius

On Style 241-243   63-64

Dio Chrysostom

Oration XII.80-83   100

Empedocles

Fragmente der Vorsokratiker, ed. Diels-Kranz, fr. 23   98

ps.-Heraclitus

Homeric Problems 26.6   66-67
— 29.4   66

Hermeias

In *Phaedrum*, ed. Couvreur,
18.20-23   122
— 33.3-4   122
— 231.6-9   78

Homer

Iliad IV.473-489   70

ps.-Longinus

On the Sublime 9.2-3   18

Olympiodorus

In *Alcibiadem*, ed. Westerink,
56.14-18   95

Philo

Quod det. pot. insid. soleat 6.15   66
Quod deus sit immutab. 27.127-128   66
Vita Mosis II.135   100-101

Plato

Phaedo 114D   35
Phaedrus 264B-E   73
— 268A-C   74-75
— 268D   73
Republic II.376E-379A   7, 34
— II.378B-D   14
— III.400D-401C   14-15
Timaeus 27C-39E   96-97
— 29D-30A   103-104
— 46C-47C   104

Plutarch

Quomodo adulescens 19E-20A   10-11

Proclus

Elements of Theology, ed. Dodds,
Prop. 140   54
In *Alcibiadem*, ed. Westerink,
18.13-19.10   84-85
— 19.9-10   123
— 42.5-43.1   123-124
In *Parmenidem*, ed. Cousin,
630.21-36   120
— 658.34-659.23   85
— 672.14-673.4   121
In *Rempublicam*, ed. Kroll,
vol. I, 11.8-13   79
— 69.23-71.17   112-113
— 71.18-86.23   109-110
— 73.11-16   47
— 73.17-22   47-48
— 74.9-76.17   49
— 76.17-86.23   49 ff.

Proclus (cont.)

— 78.18-79.14	55-56
— 81.28-83.10	53-54
— 83.12-22	57
— 83.26-84.12	56
— 85.16-26	57
— 85.26-86.23	49-50
— 159.10-22	116-117
— 162.3-19	116-117
— 163.10-172.30	110-111
— 177.4-179.32	107-109
— 198.8-24	117-118
— 198.15-19	50-51
— 202.9-205.24	118-119

In Timaeum, ed. Diehl, vol. I,

1.4-8	79
— 14.4-18.20	91-94
— 19.24-30	80, 91
— 30.11-18	41
— 60.4-11	124-125
— 87.6-15	125-126
— 132.21-27	43
— vol II, 20.19-23.16	86
— 36.20-27	87
—205.1-16	42

Quintilian

Institutio Oratoria, VIII.6.44	69

Seneca

Epistulae Morales 65.7-10	99-100

Xenophon

Memorabilia I.iv.3-10	98

3 1222 00072 7894

DISCARDED
URI LIBRARY